The Parents Manual of Sport Psychology

A PRACTICAL GUIDE TO ACHIEVING ATHLETIC SUCCESS

James I. Millhouse, Ph.D.
Clinical Sport Psychologist

ISBN: 1494285126
ISBN 13: 9781494285128

This book is dedicated to my parents who gave
my brother and I what we needed for a good start in life.
My mother Iva M. Russell Millhouse gave us unconditional
love and support in every way. My father Ernest Millhouse
showed us what can be done with creative intelligence
and a dedication to leadership in service to others.

ACKNOWLEDGEMENTS

There are several people that have been helpful to me over the years that I wish to acknowledge. I was lucky enough to have a large and supportive family including uncles, aunts and grandparents. My older brother George always had my back when I needed it. My father was extremely busy with his job and charity work so my uncles picked up the rest. My uncle Harold Russell introduced me to nature and hunting, my uncle Herbert Millhouse got me into all sorts of things including airplanes. My uncle Richard Millhouse gave me support in many ways and still rides motorcycles with me at 82 years old. My excellent professors at Michigan State in the departments of Counseling Psychology and Clinical Psychology provided me great knowledge and support, turning me into a good clinician despite myself. The great professors in Allopathic and Osteopathic Medicine at Michigan State were an inspiration and provided great role models including my dissertation director in Psychiatry, John M. Schneider, Ph.D., Chairman of Surgery Edward D. Coppola, MD, Ph.D. a gifted surgeon and scholar, and John Edwin Upledger, DO, a leader in medical research and one of the greatest healers of our time. The great German Psychoanalyst Henry Krystal, MD, whom I was lucky to serve as research assistant, gave me a strong base in psychoanalysis and taught me important things about how to help people change. Finally I wish to acknowledge Tom Adams, Ph.D. Professor of Neurophysiology in the medical school. Although I was not one even of his students, Dr. Adams took interest in me as a young research scientist, taught me how to read an electrical schematic and gave me a key to his laboratory in Giltner Hall where I spent many late nights building and testing a piece of equipment I then used in ground breaking biofeedback research. I think Dr. Adams' intellectual curiosity, unselfish commitment to science and developing students is an outstanding model of what a university professor should be. He gave more to me and the medical students than he ever knew, or would humbly ever admit, but his influence lives on in all of us and he has my eternal thanks and respect.

ABOUT THE AUTHOR

Dr. Millhouse is a licensed psychologist maintaining a private practice in Atlanta since 1985. He received a Masters in Educational Psychology in 1972 and a Ph.D. in Psychology from Michigan State University in 1982. He worked 5 years in the medical school at Michigan State teaching medical hypnosis and conducting mind/body medicine research in the Departments of Surgery, Psychiatry and the Office of Medical Education, Research and Development.

As a clinical psychologist Dr. Millhouse treats individuals suffering from issues such as depression and anxiety, but also offers assistance with non clinical requests such as family or school adjustment issues. As a Medical or Mind/Body Psychologist Dr. Millhouse consults with other doctors and provides services to patients in the areas of: stress related disorders, stress reduction, PTSD, Trauma, smoking, weight loss and substance abuse.

Dr. Millhouse has been a leader in the field of sport psychology for over 30 years. He joined the USOC Sport Psychology Registry as a Clinical Sport Psychologist in 1985 and was a founding member of the United States Association of Applied Sport Psychology, (AASP) the same year. He has taught, conducted research, and worked with athletes at Michigan State, Auburn, Georgia State and most recently at Georgia Tech for 10 years.

He has provided Mental Training for sports performance to athletes from the amateur to the professional and Olympic level in almost every sport. Hundreds of athletes and teams he has trained have achieved personal records, national titles, Olympic champion-ships and World records. He served as the Sport Psychologist for US Army elite athlete teams that set new military and Olympic records. As a result, his program was featured on NBC Nightly News during the Olympics as the next breakthrough in athletic training.

Dr. Millhouse provides performance training to teams and individuals across the country but spends most of his time work-ing with individual athletes in his Atlanta office. He was one of the first to provide performance training which included instruction in self-hypnosis and mental imagery over the telephone. This ability has allowed him to work more effectively on retainer with athletes who travel extensively. Although he works with all sports, much of his time is spent with golf and tennis. His extensive clinical back-ground combined with years of experience in sport psychology has enabled him to have great success helping professional athletes quickly escape from slumps or find the elusive key they seek that will allow them to solve a problem or go to the next level.

For more information:
Email: drmillhouse@comcast.net
letsmakewinners@gmail.com
Website: drmillhouse.com
Dr. Millhouse direct: 678 468-GOLF
(4653)

ABOUT THE BOOK

In an interview with NBC News, one of my students, Olympian Sergeant Derrick Waldroup, a member of the US Army wrestling team that set several military and Olympic records, stated "coaches have always told us to put the game face on, but it has been only recently that sport psychologists have been able to tell us step by step HOW to put the game face on." As another athlete put it, "mental training teaches you how to bring your A game, every time." That is what this book is about.

Throughout the history of sport there have always been some athletes who achieved uncommon success. In golf names like Bobby Jones and Jack Nicklaus come to mind. Some athletes were so outstanding that they are known beyond their sport such as Magic Johnson, Michael Jordan, Roger Federer, Maria Sharapova and John Smoltz to name a few.

Over the years, research studied many of the greatest athletes in the world to identify what contributed to their extraordinary ability to create success. It was found that at the higher levels of any sport there was not much difference between athletes in either physical ability or skill, but there was a big difference in the mental game between the best and the rest. It was found that there was a formula for success. For the most part, every exceptional athlete relied on the same basic set of mental procedures as part of their game plan to create success. But, just as important, they all avoided a specific set of mental operations that can interfere with performance.

Based upon this research, I compiled a list of the mental dos and don'ts from the great athletes' formula for success into a Mental Training program called Essential Concepts for Success. Over the last 25 years, I have taught this program to thousands of amateur and professional athletes.

Because the program teaches athletes to be more effective, it is really no surprise that almost every athlete has set a personal best after training. Many have won championships and titles at the regional, national, NCAA, Olympic and World level.

This book was written in two parts. The first part reviews the information provided in the Essential Concepts mental training program which identifies what the athlete needs to know about the mental game and what they need to do about it. The program also teaches athletes that their mind works mechanically, just like the rest of the body, and how to use these "mental mechanics" to create the focus the great athletes use to be their best.

Having spent a lot of time with parents over the years it became clear that a number of challenges kept repeatedly coming up. The second part of the book provides guidance with some of the more difficult or important challenges parents face such as: competition anxiety, fear of failure, lack of confidence, dealing with pressure, communicating with your athlete, working effectively with your coach and the parent role.

This book is meant to be a reference manual where you can quickly refer to a specific section to find assistance on a particular topic. But, reading the whole book will give you an excellent overview of the mental processes that impact performance and some additional ideas you may be able to use.

Please note that all contacts are held in strict confidence. Although all examples used in this book are true, names, sports, gender and venues have been changed to protect anonymity. Correct identifying data is included only with authorization.

TABLE OF CONTENTS

Chapter 1

INTRODUCTION: UNDERSTANDING THE GAME

Competition and the search for an edge

A deeper look into the nature of competition can offer clues we can use to become its master. Competition is a ubiquitous fact of life and success is determined by the quality of the competitive effort. We see it in the plant world. There is constant competition for light, water, space to grow and nutrients. The better competitors who are stronger, faster growing or just the most resilient will choke out the weaker ones or simply survive in difficult environmental conditions. In the animal world, the competition is even clearer. From the beginning at the most basic level, the bigger, stronger and more aggressive animals which were higher on the food chain would always have the animals lower on the food chain for dinner. The game became less simple when some animals began to work together and consequently were able to kill larger or more individually powerful animals. The velociraptor of the dinosaur period is thought to have been relatively intelligent and was one of the first large animals known to hunt in packs. Although they were individually no match for the larger carnivores; their mental abilities, including intelligence and ability to work together made them much more dangerous. There are numerous examples in modern animals where intelligence, channeled into strategy and cooperation, allows them to hunt more successfully than on an individual basis. The coyote is a very good example of an animal that uses intelligence to live almost invisibly among humans and employs cooperation and strategy to be a cunning hunter.

Since the earliest human history, individuals and groups have constantly had to compete for their entire existence, whether it was for survival against dangerous animals, food, shelter, belongings or the attention of a potential mate. Over time the more successful competitors have always been those who found ways to gain the advantage and rise above average. Just like the animals, size and speed were of value to humans; but it was their intelligence that kept them from being animal food and allowed them to thrive and move to the top of the food chain.

As human civilization continued to progress, it was the development of tools and weapons that became the key factor in the ability to insure the basic necessities and be victorious over other humans in battle. The Bronze Age resulted in an enormous improvement in tools and weapons that made those of the Stone Age obsolete. The Iron Age provided far more resilient tools and much stronger weapons which replaced the softer ones made of bronze. The development of better tools in the Technology Age has tremendously advanced the ability of the individual to conduct their business in the private sector just as the race for more advanced weapons has been a major goal for the military.

In warfare, the development of better weapons has been accompanied by a constant effort to improve the human factor. This effort was manifested in two ways. One way was to develop human abilities to their highest level. A good example of this is the Spartans of ancient Greece who were known to have the most highly developed physical training and psychological training of the time. The modern day example of this effort to create the most capable fighting force has resulted in military special operations commands such as the SEALS and Rangers. These modern day spec warriors have taken the formula to the next level with the most highly developed physical and psychological conditioning ever witnessed combined with the second factor of significant innovation in strategy and technique. Throughout the history of war, the most effective leaders were those who studied the methods and strategies of leaders who had gone before them. "Fortune favors the bold", a favorite saying of General George Patton is attributed to Napoleon, but he may have borrowed it from someone who preceded him.

The forgoing is important to highlight the fact that there are natural laws or dimensions common to competition in all forms at all levels. The competitor that maximizes his effort on the most dimensions will have the best chance of winning. It is no surprise to find the search for an edge in sports has evolved in an almost identical way as the quest to survive and to be the victor in combat.

Anyone involved in sports knows that there has been a never ending search for better equipment. In golf, no one hits a persimmon driver any more due to the amazing technological advancements in the new metal drivers. Safety has also increased with development of better equipment. A prime example is the air cushioned football helmets that all players use today. Better equipment can make a difference in performance which is why people invest the money to acquire it. While working for an NHL team, I was given a set of skates. When the skates were broken in so that a normal person could stand to wear them, they were too soft for the pros. The first time I put the professional skates on, my skating level increased exponentially. You don't get something for nothing though and great advancements in technology have resulted in advances in costs where a driver now costs as much as a whole set of clubs did a few years ago. Every set of equipment for a high school football player that used to cost hundreds of dollars now costs thousands. Equipment improvements have made a big difference; however the time has come where advancements in equipment are relatively minor and as long as the player has generally up to date equipment, success becomes the sole result of human factors.

In the human factor, coaches have been working to develop the highest level of technique and better strategy since the beginning of sports. In an effort to make the individual athlete more physically capable a significant advancement came with the introduction of weight training. In the recent past, practically no one did weight training until a few football teams started making it a part of their program. Soon, everyone in football did weight training just to remain competitive. Now virtually every athlete in every sport does weight training. A football coach with whom I have worked for many years and has one of the best win records in the division, was one of the first to use plyometrics for the pregame warm up. Over the last couple of years, we have seen increasing numbers of our opponents beginning to copy us.

Nutrition in sports is another human performance factor that has developed from an unknown area to an applied science. When I was growing up, the most advanced thinking in good nutrition consisted of eating a steak before a football game. As the science of nutrition developed, carbohydrate loading before a contest was introduced and everyone did it. As science continued to progress, it was found that carbohydrate loading was not the right thing to do. A few years ago research found that athletes who loaded with pure high glycemic index carbohydrates would become confused and reduce their output at a certain point; while an athlete with a correct mix of carbohydrates, protein and fat would continue to perform at a high level. These days, the most serious athletes obtain their nutrition based on a complex analysis of their nutritional needs that best addresses the task demands of their sport.

At this point in the evolution of sports performance, just like equipment, the human factors of strategy, weight training, conditioning, and nutrition have been well researched, highly developed and are employed in a fairly standard way by most serious athletes. Once again, improvements in these factors have led to higher performance in all athletes and the serious competitor is still left searching for an edge.

The Mental Edge
The best athletes in the world have shown us where the edge can be found and it is found in the mind of the athlete. More specifically, it is in how the athletes use their mind. This last frontier in sports performance is the field of Sport Psychology. The importance of the mind in sports is not a new concept to elite athletes. The golfing great Bobby Jones once said "the game of golf is

mainly played on a 5 ½ inch course, the space between your ears." Jack Nicklaus has been a major proponent of the importance of the mind in sports and has stated that he thought he may have "actually willed the ball into the cup." After winning the US Open Roger Federer stated that "at this level it is all mental." Likewise, Maria Sharapova shared her thoughts about winning a major tournament stating that "at this level, it is not about forehands and backhands." So, for those paying attention, the question is no longer does the mind matter, but how do you learn the skills to use the mind most effectively. It is abundantly clear that at the higher levels of a competition, where most athletes are always similar to each other in skills, conditioning, knowledge and equipment; it is the mental ability that determines the winner. The time has arrived where not knowing the state of art in mental technology will put an athlete at a tremendous disadvantage to another athlete who does possess this knowledge.

For a very long time, the best athletes and coaches have known the mind was important, they just did not what to do about it. One of the greatest coaches of all time, Vince Lombardi, knew the importance of the mind and worked with it at every opportunity. The problem has been that the significant development and advancements seen in all the other areas of equipment and human performance have not been available for the mental game, until now.

I previously noted the comment by Olympian Derrick Waldroup of the US Army wrestling team where he stated during an NBC Nightly News interview that the big change in the mental training available to him was a step by step process to get the mind in the right place. The "right place" is described later in this book as the Ideal Performance State which is the focus of mind and body which creates the best performance. When the interviewer, Bob Dotson, asked Derrick if the mental skills helped, he stated that "using the mental skills made me about 35% better." On a historical note, the Army team of which he was a member and assistant coach, set numerous military records and Olympic records during the 1996 Olympics. For the two previous Olympiads Derrick had been the alternate by losing to Michael Foy at Olympic trials, but learning mental skills allowed him to move to the next level and defeat Michael for the Olympic berth. Derrick finished seventh in the world while competing with a hip so messed up that he had to have surgery after the Olympics to clean it out. Training in Mental Skills did not make Derrick more "mentally tough", he was already one of the toughest men I have ever met. This can be seen by the fact that he chose to remain awake during the surgery at Bethesda to scrape out his hip. Mental Skills training helped him go beyond mentally tough to greater mental resourcefulness where he discovered the final mental tools he needed to apply all his ability to defeat the great Michael Foy for the single Olympic spot in his weight division for Greco wrestlers.

The field of Sport Psychology

At the writing of this book, almost everyone in sports has heard of sport psychology, although the field of professional study is less than 100 years old. In fact, the United States Association of Sport Psychology has only been in existence since 1985. During the last 100 years, the small number of people who began theorizing about the role of the mind in sports has grown to a professional group which has been scientifically investigating this factor. In the last 50 years or so, research has accelerated rapidly. These advancements were particularly spearheaded by efforts of the Soviet Union, their allies and a small group of other pioneers such as Lahrs-Eric Usenthal, Ph.D. of Sweden who coined the terms "mental training" and "Ideal Performance State", Coleman Griffiths, Ph.D. and the great Bruce Ogelvie, Ph.D., who many think of as the true father of Clinical Sport Psychology in the United States. In the 1970's Dr. Richard Suinn of Colorado wrote a seminal article discussing the use of VMBR (Visual Motor Behavioral Rehearsal) during this early period. VMBR is still a major technique of Sport Psychologists today but is now generally referred to as simply "imagery." A client of mine, Louise Terry, who has won several world championships in shotgun sports and also broke the world record with 498 out of 500 targets hit, used to say that the "imagery" I taught her "reinforced the fundamental actions." I would consider this a good description of VMBR impact on performance.

Sport psychologists and coaches from the Soviet Union, who once were enemies, are now our friends and colleagues, including the head of Soviet sport psychology, Albert Rodinov, Ph.D. and Anatoli Nasarenko a many time winner of Olympic gold and World championships. They have informed us that use of sport psychology was an integral part of their extremely serious sports program and a "secret protected like missile technology." Sport psychology came to the attention of the rest of the world when it was found to be a key factor in the domination of the 1976 Summer Olympic Games by the Soviets and their allies when they took most of the medals and almost all of the gold medals. Although there were accusations of steroid use, big and fast doesn't matter if you can't pull the trigger correctly. When you looked into the face of these competitors, it was unmistakable that you were looking into the eye of the tiger.

In the quest to be the best, the scholars from the Soviet Union studied every type of mental activity in sports and began identifying the thought patterns that created success and those that contributed to failure. They then taught their athletes how to focus in the most effective manner. Once their success was seen, the rest of the world began playing catch up. Research exploded to identify what thoughts, beliefs, feelings and other mental operations help an athlete train and compete at their best. This research has included studying what mental operations cause good athletes to execute poorly and conversely, what mental operations great athletes use to create success. Now it is commonly known that there is never a great physical accomplishment without a great focus of the mind. It is just as clear that the impressive loses and poor performances we see at the high levels of sport are a result of undesirable mental operations.

It was natural for sport psychology to evolve in the high level intensity of Olympic sports. At the Olympic level, the athletes are generally all extremely close in strength, skill and knowledge; so the victor will be the one who brings their best that day. Olympic athletes all have huge amounts of time, effort, money and often national resources invested in getting them there; but the single factor that will determine victory or defeat on any given day is their ability to focus and control their mind.

The Essential Concepts Mental Training Program

I entered into sport psychology ten years before the first meeting of the United States Association for Sport Psychology (AASP) in 1985. At the time there was only a handful of people in the USA talking about Sport Psychology or doing research on this topic. Over the next 35 years, through observing what worked for athletes and in communication with other professionals working in the field; it became clear to me that there was a certain body of knowledge and mental skills that every athlete needed to know in order to make the most of their resources.

Although the Soviets were not giving up any information about their sport psychology programs in the early days, once the rest of the world saw what their athletes could do, research began in earnest. Some of the research duplicated understanding of mental processes from general psychology, but of major import was the study of why some athletes performed consistently better or reached a higher level than others. It was found that athletes who were outstanding performers such as Magic Johnson, Michael Jordan, Jack Nicklaus, Bobby Jones, Wayne Gretzky and other great athletes and coaches performed mental operations or engaged in different thoughts than their contemporaries who were equally fit and skilled, but less accomplished.

Once it was determined what the superior athletes did to create better or more consistent results I began developing a mental training program to teach other athletes what mental processes created exceptional results and how integrate these processes into their training program. Some of the knowledge that was incorporated into the mental training program was drawn from research in general psychology and educational psychology. This area of knowledge includes research in human learning theory, operant conditioning, classical conditioning, Neurolinguistic Programming (NLP), modeling and a host of other areas of knowledge regarding basic mental function. I became exposed to this information during my Bachelors of Science degree in Psychology and my Masters of Science degree in Educational Psychology at Michigan State University. A large part of our educational system is organized around these mental rules or learning principles which form the substance of classes I taught in Educational Psychology at Michigan State. The mental functioning of all athletes is based upon these mental rules and proper or improper use of them has an enormous impact on effectiveness.

Another source of information included in the Mental Skills Training Program was drawn from the results of mind/body research in the medical setting. Although I am a psychologist, during my entire Ph.D. program at Michigan State University, I worked for the Allopathic and Osteopathic medical schools in various departments including Psychiatry, Surgery and the Office of Medical Education, Research and Development. During this time, I served as the research assistant to Edward D. Coppola, M.D, Ph.D. who is one of the great surgeons of our time. Dr. Coppola was chairman of the surgery department in part because he achieved abnormally good results in surgery and was a phenomenal scholar. The goal of the research was to identify and investigate every instance in the literature where psychology appeared to have an impact in medicine and surgery from the earliest medical records to the current time. The data studied included the impact of pre and post operative information given to patients, mesmerism, medical hypnosis, self-hypnosis, all forms of meditation, yoga and even things that seemed on the fringe such as faith healing, shamanism and the like. No stone was left unturned.

One result of the research was a much deeper level of understanding of the mechanisms involved in the connection between the mind and body. Another major finding was that there was a set of specific mental operations that were consistently found in most of the disciplines studied. Although some of the disciplines practiced in different parts of the world included spiritual or conceptual differences from others, at the root of the disciplines were many of the same mental procedures that operated in exactly the same way. It was discovered that there is a set of strict operational procedures relating to mental functioning and mind/body connections that are common to all humans in just about any task. Two things became clear. First, the mind operates mechanically, just like the rest of the body and when you use your mind in a certain way; you will always get the same result. And secondly, that there is a tremendous amount of influence the mind can have on physical health and sickness in ways that we now understand. For ease of discussion, I decided to group this set of mental procedures by which the mind operates and process by which it impacts the physical body under the term "mental mechanics."

Some of the knowledge gained in the research was integrated into treatments for diseases such as cancer where mental imagery was found to almost double parts of the immune system function as noted in a research paper by John M. Schneider, Ph.D. in 1982. Other information obtained from this and related mind-body research is routinely used in medical treatment and surgical procedures today.

In addition, some of the findings that specified the processes by which the mind impacted physical body operations were found to be directly relevant to performance in sports. Based on this information, I began development of a mental training program that taught athletes that their mind operated mechanically, just like the rest of their body, and how to use this knowledge to implement the mental processes of the great athletes. It was easy for athletes to understand that the mind was just like any other machine, such as a smart phone or automobile, where once you learned how it worked, you could use it in a more productive way to achieve your goals.

This application of mental mechanics was first compiled into the current program in a mental skills program I created for the Junior Olympic Athlete Development Program (JOAD) that was provided to young tennis players. It was later revised while working with the United States Army World Class Athlete Program (WCAP). The revised program seemed to work well with the Army team that used it to set new Military and US Olympic records and has been found to be very effective with few revisions as a training program since that time. Over the last 20 years it has been proven over and over again with junior, collegiate, professional and Olympic athletes that understanding how their mind worked allowed them to compete more consistently and reach higher goals, sometimes more than they had ever imagined possible.

Sport Psychology Services
As I mention in several places in this book, Sport Psychologists can widely differ in their training and abilities and offer a wide range of services, but it may be helpful to use my program as a fairly basic template. There are generally two types of services that I provide as a Sport Psychologist. These are different than the clinical psychology services that I provide to patients that seek my care for mental health reasons. Athletes are not patients

and are not considered mentally ill or mentally deficient. Mental training provides athletes knowledge that is sometimes not naturally intuitive and is not likely to be obtained from a source other than mental training, but consistently works. A large part of my time is devoted to teaching athletes who do not have any particular "problem" the fundamental mental skills contained in this program that they can use to reach higher levels of performance. For many years, I consulted with a football team where I would work with them off the field to teach them the mental skills and then meet with them a short time just before the game to help them use the mental skills to get into the best focus to play. The team was extraordinarily successful with almost constant entry into the playoffs. This is a standard way to work with a team, but other patterns have been successful as well.

Over the years coaches have requested that I provide a mental focusing drill right before they took the floor without previous mental training. This has happened when I was working with a few individual athletes on the team, but not with the team as a group, and had not even gone over the Essential Concepts with the team. These were not dumb coaches but very highly respected at the Division One and professional level. I told the coaches that I did not advise this procedure, but the coaches wanted it anyway, so I complied thinking something was better than nothing. The procedure I used was to help the athlete remember and bring into the present moment their IPS. Although this was not the methodology that I would suggest, the results have been good 100% of the time. In all cases the coaches wanted the team to start well, and so far, every team has started better than any time in recent memory. Still, the risk is high for this type of procedure and

I do not suggest it, particularly with a provider that is relatively new to the situation or with little history that you can evaluate. I significantly prefer teaching the team the relevant information in several sessions prior to a game and then providing a focusing drill just before the contest.

The other way I spend a great amount of time with athletes is in the Clinical Sport Psychologist role where I teach them how to overcome some difficulty they are having. The more common requests include such things as not playing as well in a game as in practice, problems with various forms of performance anxiety and recovery from slumps. Over the years I have been so successful in showing athletes how to get out of slumps that I have acquired the nickname of Dr. Slump in baseball circles. Slumps are easier to deal with than one might think when you understand the mental mechanics involved. Athletes stuck in slumps have frequently returned to normal in one to three sessions. As an added benefit, once an athlete has learned how they get into slumps, and how to use mental skills to get back to normal, they tend to be much more resilient to slumps in the future.

The term Sport Psychology encompasses the entire body of knowledge, research and training activities in this field. Individuals who offer some type of Sport Psychology training will be referred to in this book as Sport Psychologists or by the generic label of "providers." The term "mental training" is used generically in this book to denote any type of Sport Psychology training which includes providing information crucial to performance, as well as specific training in mental skills. Useful information can be obtained from books, but books have limitations, and a mental coach is helpful, and often necessary to help the athlete use the information, just as it is with physical technique in sport skills. It is important to understand that there can be large differences between the types of individuals offering mental training, and the information they provide. These differences are discussed in greater detail in the chapter on choosing a sport psychologist.

Chapter 2

ESSENTIAL CONCEPTS: INTRODUCTION

Sport Psychology and Performance

Over 35 years of working with athletes on performance issues and training athletes in the use of mental skills, it became clear that there was a set of fundamental knowledge about how the mind works in sports that virtually every athlete needed to know. An athlete using this knowledge of mental mechanics, and the related mental skills, can more easily avoid many common difficulties such as inconsistency and slumps, train more effectively and compete more consistently at a higher level. Because the need for this knowledge is universal, I developed the Essential Concepts training program that explains the relevant mental mechanics and teaches athletes how to use them correctly.

Some individual athletes or teams come to me with something specific in mind. One sprinter on a Division 1 track team was the fastest man in his state, although he was usually last out of the blocks. Once I taught him how to get out of the blocks more quickly, his speed won him a shot at the Olympic team. Frequently, baseball or softball players will ask me to get them out of slumps or over other problems that have developed in their game. Golfers frequently request help with the yips or problems with losing some part of their game. Some teams also request specific things such as a basketball team that primarily wanted to increase a weak free throw percentage. Some uses for mental skills are common across all teams in the same sport. For example, getting out of the blocks quickly is almost always a topic I introduce to swim teams because it is quick to learn and almost all swimmers can use it. However, many teams request a general program to teach them the mental skills they need to be at their best and how to get focused to be their best in each game. Regardless of the request, the essential concepts are very much involved in the solution.

Although reading this book will not make you a sport psychologist, I believe it will give you a good understanding of the basic concepts central to sports that you can use to help your athlete. If you are reading this book because your child is in one of my training programs, the information will help you understand the advanced thoughts and behaviors your child is developing, and make it easier for you to support the changes.

The Performance Quotient

It may be useful to introduce the concept of the Performance Quotient (PQ). We are all familiar with the IQ or Intelligence Quotient, which is supposed to measure how smart we are. Recently in the context of business consulting, author Dan Goleman introduced the notion of the Emotional Quotient (EQ). The EQ is a measure of how well the individual can handle the emotional challenges presented in the business environment. It is said in business that your IQ will get you hired but your EQ will determine how successful you will be.

The PQ represents a measure of the amount and accuracy of sport psychology knowledge and mental skills that an athlete can bring to bear in the sport. The higher the PQ, the more the athlete will be able to make effective use of their physical ability, sport specific skills and resources during training and competition. In other words, a high PQ gives you more "bang for the buck." Over the years, the athletes with a high PQ have always been the ones who were more consistent, more coachable and known to be the "clutch" players that everyone wants on their team.

It bears repeating that although mental training has been developed for application in a sport context, a high PQ is universally valuable for all ages in all things. It has been said that a high PQ indicates one's relative ability to effectively take action, which really is the basis for advancement or success in any area of life. It is interesting, that the increased abilities of an individual with a high PQ makes it easier to handle the mental and emotional challenges related to the EQ, and also enable a higher level of concentration and emotional control that would facilitate doing well on a test resulting in a higher IQ. I once worked with a high school age elite performing artist who used the skills to let their abilities flow in musical performances. As a side benefit, he found that his SAT scores improved because he could get in a more resourceful state to take the test.

Developing a high PQ is of particularly great importance for the middle or high school athlete outside of sports. It is at this time that the belief in one's own abilities as well as mental habits and mental operations are developed. The child will depend on these habits the rest of their life and the quality of these abilities will partially determine the quality of their life.

Research has shown that high school or college students with a high PQ are better able to handle the stress imposed by an increasingly busy and demanding school environment. Many students report an improvement in grades, or that good grades come more easily because they are able to focus more powerfully with higher levels of concentration for studying and taking tests. Performance skills an athlete may use to handle stress and get into best focus of the mind/body state to compete can also be used to take an exam, make a presentation and even work more effectively on a project.

It is the same in the adult world where mental skills have been used by attorneys to make a convincing case in court or by people in business to make an effective presentation. Adult actors and musicians have used the same skills to perform and artists have been using them for years to be creative. Mental focusing skills can be used to adjust energy level by an athlete to relax or to get more energy toward the end of a competition. Others have used this technique to get to sleep more easily or achieve a deeply relaxed state, which is a cornerstone of stress reduction. The same mental imagery skills an athlete uses to overcome bad competition habits, or remove technical problems, can also be used to change undesirable habits and problem behaviors such as overeating, smoking, drinking and using drugs. In the area of personal coaching for executives the mental skills from sport psychology now comprise some of the highest level and most important information imparted in an executive coaching program.

The three components of success

Performance in sports is determined by the level that an athlete has mastered the three components of success. Athletes and teams differ in the amount they have maximized the three components, but the goal of a coach or athlete is to have all three at the highest level.

The first component is the level of physical ability that can be brought to the competition. Strength and endurance has been one of the major training goals in athletics for a long time. From early days of sport until present day, coaches have spent large amounts of time focusing on building strength and endurance. A high level of this component is considered a necessary but not sufficient tool for success. Recently, some of the more advanced and successful coaches have included plyometrics as an advanced pregame warm up program to better prepare the athlete physically for activity.

The second component necessary for success is knowledge of the game, strategy and highly developed sport skills. Information to help the athlete maximize their ability in these areas is mainly derived from coaching. Some information is learned through books and handouts from the coach, but the refinement of skill to the level desired for competition almost always has to come from coaching information and feedback specific to the efforts of the individual athlete. Even in a team sport, the individual athlete is responsible for working as hard as necessary to develop their physical skills and knowledge of what is necessary to get to the desired level. This second component has also been a primary focus for coaching since the beginning of sport.

The third component is the mental ability to pull the trigger on the best focus for execution to use the first two components most effectively. Coaches and athletes have always known that mental focus was important. They have always wanted the right mental state to be present in competition; but until recently, the ability to adjust the mental state to the level and quality most needed has been very elusive. Many attempts have been made by coaches to get their athletes on focus but often the attempts did not produce everything the coach hoped for, were at times ineffective and sometimes even detrimental to the competition and the athlete. It can be hard to hit the target when you are shooting in the dark. For example, negative coaching attitudes have helped some athletes by challenging them, but been very detrimental to most others. Advancements in sport psychology have now made mental training available which provides the tools to accomplish this task more effectively.

The first two factors have been developed to the extent that most athletes have access to most of the same knowledge which levels the playing field. In most of the competitions we see these days, although several of the athletes have sufficient resources of factor one and factor two to win, the actual victor will be the one with the superior mental program.

The Essential Concepts mental training program includes three areas of knowledge that provide valuable guidance on how to operate the mind more effectively, whether it's training, competing, studying, presenting in class or taking a test. I have labeled these areas of knowledge; Key Conceptual Knowledge, Key Operative Knowledge and Mental Skills, collectively referred to simply as Mental Training.

This breakdown of information has stood the test of time for many years. When we see a great victory, we can always find that these patterns were all present at a high level. To the converse, when we witness failure and loss of a contest, we can usually find one of these areas not adequately developed or not executed at a sufficiently competent level. Very frequently, especially at high levels, we find a big loss caused or associated with a significant mental component breakdown.

For your convenience, each section of the Essential Concepts program is covered in a separate chapter that will make it easier to access the concepts for review. The information discussed in all three chapters comprising the Essential Concepts Program is directed toward enabling the athlete to use all the resources they have developed in factors 1 and 2 when they need them the most. The rest of the chapters which discuss specific issues will frequently refer back to information covered in the program for tools to create solutions.

Chapter 3

KEY CONCEPTUAL KNOWLEDGE

Introduction

Key Conceptual Knowledge contains information about what the athlete needs to understand about the mental mechanics used by the mind in sport opposed to the next section which describes more of what they need to do. Everyone has the ability to think anything at any given point in time but habits often determine what is in the content of our thoughts. After each concept is explained, the rationale for the recommended thought and focus may make it easier to make the most effective choice. All humans resist all change to a varying degree. The thoughts and responses we already have in place may seem most natural because they are habits and are familiar. It can be expected to take extra thought and effort to make the changes but soon the changes that require extra thought and effort will become automatic, just like the old and less productive patterns. All other sport psychology information and every mental operation done by an athlete is built upon these basic mental mechanics so it is very important to understand and execute them correctly. Experience has shown that the more successful athletes will probably know and use some of these concepts correctly, but until they have had comprehensive mental training, they usually have some gaps that are costly to them. There are differences found among athletes and your child might be an exception on some dimensions. For example, some athletes use negative coaching effectively, but most are harmed by it so you need to evaluate your athlete's understanding of the concepts and experiment to find the best way to explain them and determine what works best for your athlete. Again, everything presented here has been shown to work for most athletes in most sports for many years so it is a good place to start.

The Ideal Performance State

The Ideal Performance State (IPS) is the single most important concept in the mental game. Of course, if there are glaring deficiencies in things such as fitness, skills, knowledge or debilitating anxiety, those things take precedence as areas needing immediate attention, but such problems notwithstanding, the most important part of the mental game impacting performance is the IPS. The IPS designation stands for the state of the mind and body the athlete is in when everything is working for him and he is at his best. The IPS is often confused with the Zone because they mean almost the same thing, but not quite. The concept of the Zone has taken on numerous meanings over the years, and as a result the meaning has become muddled. It has been always believed that you cannot get into the zone anytime you wish and that it just happened. This has been the case in the past, but it is now known that developing the IPS creates most if not all of the benefits of the Zone and at some point the two concepts may become indistinguishable.

The Zone has been understood as one specific condition which is present or not and although the IPS is the road to the

Zone, it is not the Zone. Unlike the Zone, the IPS is a state that an athlete learns to develop gradually over time and is present in variable amounts at different times, depending on the ability of the athlete to get there at the moment. The IPS is to some extent different for different athletes and may be somewhat different for the same athlete in different situations, in the same sport or across sports. Usually it is pretty much the same though, and the goal for the athlete is to determine what their version of the IPS is for specific situations, such as training, competition and in different sports. For instance, the IPS for an athlete playing linebacker in football will be somewhat different from the same athlete's IPS for shooting free throws in basketball. On the other hand, their IPS for shooting free throws in practice will be the same for the game and frequently this is a goal for an athlete to get into the same IPS in both situations. Frequently it is easier for them to get in it during practice and the challenge is to get there in a game. Once the components of the IPS are identified, the athlete can then determine what they need to do to get there.

When a person is in the IPS, there is a specific constellation of events present in his mind and body. The mental part of the IPS includes specific thoughts, beliefs, feelings, expectations, circulating neurotransmitters and brain wave patterns. The physical part of the zone, if we artificially separate the mind and body, includes the state of relaxation or tension in the body, circulating hormones and neurotransmitters including more or less adrenalin, blood sugar level, respiration rate, heart rate and general state of arousal.

Maybe you can remember seeing an athlete who could do very well in practice but not perform at the same level in competition.

When we stop and think about it, we can probably remember in our own performances, and those of others, when doing very well seemed easy and everything seemed to flow or work out right. At these times we made the right choices, the execution of our skills went well, such as our backhand or drive being "on" or our stroke or stride feeling almost effortless.

On the other hand, maybe you can remember times when the same athlete who had the same abilities could not perform at the same level. Maybe a forehand that was usually totally reliable was just not working that day or maybe driving or putting the ball just was not up to the usual quality. What is the difference? Excepting situations where an opponent physically interferes with execution such as tackling or blocking a pass, the reason for a difference in performance is due to a difference in state.

Many an athlete has been frustrated when they could play well in practice but did not perform as well in a game. Golfers commonly struggle with the situation where a shot that was working well on the range was not there in the game. This is so prominent in golf because the game is extremely responsive to changes in state. Most athletes do not know that once an athlete has reliably executed a particular skill such as a forehand or specific golf shot, the reason they can execute reliably over and over is because they have an execution program stored in their brain. The program stays in the brain for a very long time which is the reason we often see a golfer executing quite well in the first round out after a long lay off. Neuroscience has recently discovered that when learning occurs actual physical structures are created in the brain that are reinforced and elaborated with continued use. After a program has been stored, executing the skill effectively is a result of merely accessing the program, just like accessing a program on a computer. On a computer, if you hit the right keys you will access the program you want, every time. The mind is the same where the key to accessing the program is the mind/body state. When an athlete gets into the right state, this creates effective access to the program and they get the highest level of execution, practically every time. In other words, the access to a mental program is through creating the proper state, which is usually the IPS.

For the golfer who has a good shot on the range, the challenge is to achieve the same state on the golf course and the shot will be there. The problem for athletes who cannot take their skills from practice to competition is that they unwittingly change state. So when an athlete in competition loses a skill, the way to get it back is through learning how to get back into the correct state to access the skill program.

To clear up some potential confusion, let me explain this another way. The execution program is tied to the state present when it is created. If a golfer was always scared to death during a game, if they practiced scared to death, the skills developed would transfer nicely. However, that is not how most people practice and develop skills. The most productive and effective way to practice and develop skills is in the IPS. So, it follows that a golfer would then seek to develop the IPS on the course when replication of the skill was desired.

Although many coaches and even sport psychologists do not realize it, almost all mental skills training is directed toward recognizing and accessing the Ideal Performance State. Over the years when coaches have told athletes to "put the game face on", what they really meant, although they probably did not realize it at the time, was "get into the IPS."

The steps for an athlete to begin working with these concepts is first to become aware of what comprises the state they are creating when things are going well. Mainly they would start by assessing their thoughts, emotions and the level of tension and relaxation in their body. Once this state is identified, a major goal of the athlete is to get back into this state, and maintain it, each time they compete. Most of the conceptual and operational knowledge discussed in this basic program can be seen as tools the athlete can use to both identify the IPS, and then develop it when they are preparing to compete. Although this procedure may sound simple, the process of identifying the components of the IPS, and then having the ability to create those components in competition to enter into the IPS, can be quite challenging. This is where the assistance of a good mental coach in the form of a qualified Sport Psychologist can be quite helpful.

In summary, the IPS is the constellation of everything going on inside an athlete when the athlete is at their best. Everything discussed as part of the Essential Concepts has an impact on the IPS which can be seen as the focus an athlete wants to be in at least in times of practice of the unit of execution that will be desired in competition.

For the most part, I believe fear has no place in the IPS and a substantial part of my work is to help take the fear out of competition. However, there are many different feelings and attitudes that may be a part of the IPS for different athletes. Eventually, most of the components of the IPS we discuss in this book should become second nature or standard operating procedure for your athlete. When it gets to that point for an athlete, they usually are able to reduce their competition focus to some simple guiding thoughts based upon their beliefs and view of the world that maintains their IPS focus. For example, one of our Olympic athletes, Jessica Long, stated that her formula for success, part of her IPS focus, is to "work real hard and never give up." Katlin Farrington, American winner of the Olympic Half-Pipe, stated that she competed with hope to be on the podium but never thought she would win the gold. She won the gold due to a total focus on the process of executing her run, as opposed to any focus on winning the gold. Generally all the descriptions of the IPS of champions include the Essential Concepts maximized and some type of guiding intention that focuses them on the process in an optimal way.

Throughout the remainder of the book you may want to keep in mind that this is, for the most part, our ultimate goal. If the IPS is achieved, results take care of themselves. Regarding factor three, the ability to pull the trigger, we cannot do any more than this to compete most effectively, and to appropriately honor ourselves and our supporters, we really do not want to do any less. As one Olympian said, "there is no shame in ending up fourth." I would add that if an athlete has given it all they had, that there is never any shame no matter where they ended up in the final ranking. I would argue that understanding the IPS gives us the formula to compete at our best with no regrets. This is not the last time we will discuss or elaborate the IPS, but I hope this discussion gets us off to a good start.

Execution focus

The second concept essential to understand and use is the proper focus for execution. There are two major components to a proper execution focus. The first component is the time focus. All great execution is created while in a present focus. Although some athletes may have had some success while focusing on the past or the future, the result is always a mere fraction of what could be obtained when focused correctly. Many of the very poor executions, mistakes and losses in a competition are a result of the athlete focusing on concerns from past performances or worrying about what will happen in the future if they do not compete well or even if they do. To expect good execution, the athlete must be focused in the present time frame.

One basketball player came to my office because he had lost his shot, which is not an uncommon experience for basketball players. Usually, coaches tell a player to keep shooting in the hope that they will start hitting. This is called "the shooters mentality." This has been the advice for years because it is the only answer coaches had, other than to correct any technique problems. If it is a technique problem, or something physical such at tiredness in their legs, it is easily recognized and fixed immediately. But, when no technique or physical problems are present and players go into a slump, it is mental, which is usually the case when a player who has had a good shot stops hitting. The great basketball player Larry Bird was great at making a shot when everything was not perfect, even when he was falling down. When a player misses a shot, they are certainly doing something physically wrong, which causes the miss, but the reason they do the wrong physical thing is due to a change in mental operations. When the mental approach of this player under discussion was analyzed, it was found that when he went to shoot, he was partially thinking about how important it was to make the shot. This is a future focus that not only took his attention off what needed to be done to execute correctly, but also added the stress of performance considerations. The stress changed his physiology slightly which created enough physical tension to disturb smooth execution of his shot and make him miss. In other words, it took him out of his IPS causing him to miss. Once he understood the mistake he was making, and that he needed to stay in a present focus, he immediately started hitting again in practice and games.

A baseball player came to me in a hitting slump. He was a great hitter and a major part of the offense of his team. To make matters worse, it was just before the beginning of a championship series. You may already be anticipating the problem. Analysis of his hitting process found that he was going to the plate demanding himself to get a hit, upset about his recent performances and thinking "oh no, I hope it doesn't happen again". Needless to say, his IPS was blown by focusing on both the past and the future and by stressing himself out of the physiological state where he commonly was when he performed at a high level. The player was first shown how he was getting himself out of his IPS. A pre-hitting routine was then created that put him into his IPS that included the correct time focus, level of arousal and other correct IPS components. The result was that he immediately started hitting like he was before the slump, actually hit above his best average during the championship series and was named MVP. The execution focus is one of the most important components of the IPS to have under control.

In a recent Olympics a pair was skating in the finals, which would be their last competition. The commentator stated "this is their last Olympics but to win a gold they would have to have a score significantly higher than had ever been achieved before," and he wondered "how you could skate with that pressure." This is where philosophy may come to play in choice of focus. The focus chosen by the skaters was to go all out, even throwing in something very hard at the end, leaving nothing on the ice. They did not win gold, I think they may have won a bronze medal though, but they definitely did earn the respect of everyone in attendance for not holding back and going down swinging. That focus, as part of their IPS, allowed them to bring their best, which resulted in the best performance they could have created and all they or anyone intelligent could have asked for.

There are actually a lot of things that can go into the correct execution focus in addition to the time factor. In the example above, the skaters chose the focus of totally going for it without regard to the fact that they could not win the gold. The focus they chose eliminated distractions and led to a uncompromised execution focus that got the job done. In a recent Olympics, medal winning bobsled driver Elana Meyers was asked in an interview "how do you hold on to the lead." She gave a perfect response from the view of a sport psychologist when she said "It's not about holding on to a lead, it's about attacking every run." Protecting a lead has been the reason many athletes have lost a competition, it seems logical, but it usually results in substandard play.

Feelings
Feelings before and during execution can also have a positive or negative influence on the IPS. Athletes are mostly the same

regarding the emotions that contribute most to the IPS, but do differ occasionally to some extent. It needs to be determined for each athlete what feelings help them perform at their highest level. You can begin with the general guidelines that are best for most athletes, such as focusing in the moment, generally positive feelings, but then look further to identify the specific feelings which contribute to the right focus as part of the IPS for each individual athlete. Coaches have always known that feelings were important and generally tried to get their athletes into what the coaches thought were the best emotions.

In football, which is an aggressive sport, many coaches have tried to get their athletes angry and hostile, which worked to some extent. However, even if a football player needed to be experiencing angry and hostile emotions, sometimes the coaches would get them too intense, resulting in offside and personal foul penalties. In this case, even if the players used hostile feelings to bring their best, they needed to be at the right level of them. On the other hand, having coached football for over 15 years, I have seen many players that needed to be focused in emotions different or in addition to the correct level of hostility such as confidence, commitment to the task, feelings regarding the team or others that were specific to them. Continuing with the example of football, different positions tend to require different feelings and focus. Defensive linemen tend to use extreme hostility and aggression where quarterbacks generally need a more calm emotional focus due to the need for concentration and quick but complicated thinking.

Research in sport psychology has made it clear that we must not assume that all players in a specific sport and position need to feel the same thing. The key is to identify what feelings are present in their IPS and help the athlete create those feelings when they are needed. Many coaches have traditionally believed that hostility and aggression were the most desirable emotions in most sports, but this is not always true. Research has found that many athletes do even better when experiencing positive emotions such as fun, enjoyment, or other things that motivate them rather than just the emotion to fight against or attack. This is especially true for young athletes, even in the aggressive sports such as football and martial arts.

The sports of tennis and golf can provide us some good examples to delve deeper into the specifics of this concept. These days it is generally accepted by good coaches that in the early stages of learning these sports it is important for the player to have fun. When a player has shown some aptitude or talent for the sport, many times coaches and parents have decided that it was time to "get serious" about the sport. Unfortunately, they conceived that getting "serious about the sport and working hard" had to include a reduction of the pleasure the athlete experienced during training and competition. This is not necessarily true and has frequently created problems including the athlete enjoying the sport less, not wanting to practice and having increased negative emotions and stress associated with competition. This is the main reason many talented kids have under performed and even left the sport, because it "wasn't fun anymore."

One of the many superior ways to treat the situation of training is to keep it fun while working for the goals and eliminate negative consequences of mistakes. This does not mean to not feel displeased with mistakes, or not use mistakes for additional information, just to not invest mistakes with an inordinate amount of negative emotion. For example, in a tennis drill where the player is trying to hit cones with a shot, rather than respond negatively to misses and possibly challenging the player's motivation, a coach can create an atmosphere of fun and reward for the cones that are hit. The player does not want to miss the cone, may be disappointed they missed it and there is no benefit to be gained by punishing them further for a miss.

The following true story is a particularly egregious example of destructive coaching that ignored the feeling component. A family friend who played tennis was asked to help coach a very talented young girl. In a misguided attempt to motivate the girl to try harder, he took the prized doll collection on to the court and told her every time she made a mistake that she would lose a doll and never see it again. The young girl was soon a sobbing pile of mush on the court and never wanted to play again. She did try to play at a future time to obtain some scholarships, but was never able to get over the emotionally damaging incident.

In another example, Kevin Brown, an excellent elite gymnastics coach was working with some top level girls at an elite camp where I was coaching. He was working with them in a drill which required them to swing up very high on the boy's high bar, which is not a competition event for girls. The girls were all scared and due to the fear were not putting out the effort they were capable of creating. Rather than criticize them for lack of effort or cowardice, Kevin told them that he would buy a Coke for the girl who swung up the highest. The result was that the girls immediately started swinging higher, scaring themselves and laughing about it.

Although the inclusion of fun in my handout for the JOAD tennis program may seem simplistic at first glance, it is important not to dismiss concepts that may seem simple. The purpose in the handout was to generally get the kids away from frequent negative emotions about what they could not do, negative emotions are known to inhibit learning and development, as well as generate positive emotions. However, Lydia Ko, a 16 year old professional golfer who has been recently finishing at or near the top in professional tournaments commented during a tournament where she was near the top, "It is so much fun to drive the ball where it is really taking off on the ground." She usually seems happy and plays golf at the level of a seasoned professional, so it seems to work for her.

I always suggest to my athletes that they watch as much of the Olympics as possible, including other sports different from their main interest. The purpose, of course, is for them to find clues in the experience of great athletes regarding how they function and focus in the highest pressure venue that exists. Bodie Miller, one of out greatest ski racers, stated that the feeling he would reach for was "some combination of aggression and relaxation." Some athletes report feeding on the energy of the Olympics drives them to be better. Other athletes say that they try to put the emotions of being at the Olympics into a dissociated part of their mind so feelings do not intrude into their consciousness and interfere with their concentration and thereby disturb their IPS. However, it is better for the athlete to change their mind so they do not have fears or concerns to control because fear has a way of breaking through at inopportune times during competition. This can be seen clearly in individual competition sports such as figure skating where a faltering of focus has immediate and usually disastrous consequences that are evident to everyone. It is much better to find a way of thinking about the situation where no fear is created.

As previously mentioned, although we generally cannot say 100% about anything, one thing that is perfectly clear for almost every athlete is that fear has no place in competition. We talk about fear in several areas of this book regarding how it is created and what to do about it, but the main message is that you do not want to tolerate its existence in your athlete. Just telling an athlete not to be afraid usually does not do much. You need to find a way to help them understand the situation so that they will not be afraid or find some other way to deal with it.

Almost every accomplished athlete will tell you that they want to be fearless. This may be one of your greater challenges in helping your athlete develop the best focus, in other words, the IPS, but few things are as important. Ideally, you want the fearlessness to go to the deepest part of their mind and emotions. Many times we see athletes who have dealt with this at a superficial level, but when it is time to compete in the big contests, deep unresolved fears come out and destroy their chances to perform at the level of which they are capable. In a clear example of how all the essential concepts work together to form the IPS, we had an Olympic skater in the past who on paper had the edge on everyone, but when it was time to go for the gold they made mistakes on things they had done right hundreds of times. I have never met that athlete but it was very clear that deeply hidden fears regarding outcome, or something performance related, came out and destroyed their IPS such that they were not able to put on the performance they were capable of creating. It was known that if they had a bad short program, then they would have a good long program. If they had a great short program, then they usually would falter on the long. A very good guess would be that they had fear related to outcome which came out and interfered with their IPS when they had a real shot at the gold. It was really a shame because everyone knew that if they just skated up to their ability, the gold was practically in their pocket.

Unfortunately in the last Olympics we saw more situations where skaters had fear at a deep level that was not addressed effectively. Their fear interfered with their ability to execute and show the world what their hard work had made them capable of producing. I think it is profoundly sad when athletes put so much work into their hopes and dreams, only to have them derailed by unresolved fear that could be abolished if they only understood how to do it. Each athlete will have a way that works best for them to deal with fear, it just needs to be found. Bobsledding is a dangerous sport with a heavy sled and occupants hurtling down the ice at nearly one hundred miles an hour. Elana Meyers the American bobsled driver stated in an interview that "there is always that little bit of fear at the top, but you just push through it and go." We know that worked for her because she drove well and won a medal. However, each athlete has to develop the methodology that works best for them to deal with fear, or any other emotion, that can impact their focus.

As with most things discussed in this book, this discussion is not intended to provide you the knowledge of what your athlete needs or the specific solution that will best enable their efforts to develop, but to provide you direction to obtain these answers. Even at the highest levels, what could be considered the most serious situations, such as the Olympics or World Championships, most athletes report some type of positive emotion or positive experience of the challenge works best and that negative emotions or fear almost always results in a reduced ability to execute. We have spent a lot of time discussing what we do not want, that is fear, but the other side of the coin is to be engaged in emotions that create what we do want. Whatever the feeling is, whether it is love of the sport, passion, or something else, it is important for the athlete to be aware of the feeling that enables them and learn to experience that feeling to the exclusion of all others during the process of creating their performance.

Almost all the successful Olympic athletes talk in the interviews about the focus they used to get the job done. Sometimes athletes have spoken of using fear of losing to drive their practices, but fear in competition disrupts the IPS at so many levels that it makes doing our best impossible. One Olympic skater stated that their formula for the right combination of emotions was to "love it and let go of fear." Each athlete has to find the feeling that leads them to create their best expression of their abilities and learn how to create it exclusively and consistently. Some skaters speak of passion as their dominate emotion and others talk about creating beauty. That is one half of the combination that is irreplaceable, the other half is the elimination of debilitating fear. The first thing to do is choose the desired emotion and focus, the next part, making it happen, is usually a challenge. When I am working with an athlete, I usually go to the Mental Skills part of the program for the resources to create and maintain the focus as needed.

Perfectionism

The concepts of perfection and perfectionism are encountered by every athlete and although dealing with them inappropriately can be problematic, the most important reason for including them in this discussion is that an understanding of them can make things run more efficiently. In the case of a beginning golfer, the professional first teaches the student how to stand, how to set up to the ball, how to hold the club properly and the mechanics of the swing. The student then tries to replicate what they were shown and the professional makes corrections so the student will perform the actions as perfectly as possible. The student then practices with the intent to consistently replicate what they were taught as perfectly as possible. Subsequent visits to the pro constitute correcting deviations that have entered into the student's execution that bring his technique back to executing as precisely or perfectly what the pro intended and adding new skills that also need to be learned as precisely as possible. Essentially we all go through a phase while learning a sport where we are all perfectionists attempting to replicate what we have been shown as perfectly as possible.

As we progress, perfection in technique still remains a goal but other goals become equally and sometimes more important than perfect technique. At some point, effectiveness becomes a more prominent goal than perfect technique. For example, a football team may be told before a game to "let it fly" and mistakes or less than perfect execution are of secondary importance to the goal of reading and responding quickly with full commitment. A receiver may still try to remember to "look the ball into his hands" but the emphasis will be catching the ball any way he can, holding on to the ball and thirdly, gaining yardage, if possible.

It is important to avoid perfectionism. Aristotle once described perfectionism as "the attempt to become more than human". Because athletes begin learning their sport by trying to replicate what they are shown by the coach as perfectly as possible, they may become confused at times about when it is best to trade the perfect for the good. It is important to have the correct balance in these concepts as leaning too much toward just getting it done without great technique can also retard development of the ability to perform most effectively. Leaning too much the other way can lead to perfectionism. Although we frequently see more sloppy technique that puts limits on achievement, some of the more talented, intelligent and conscientious athletes can get into perfectionism which results in limiting their achievement in another way. These athletes will tend to focus on technique to the extent that they experience anger or other unhappy emotions, damaging their IPS and create a downward cycle of quality in execution. Helping these athletes hold perfection in the proper perspective is an important part of learning how to be successful. It is important to not sacrifice the good for the perfect.

To be successful in the competitive environment of today an athlete must be driven to become more perfect, but it is important to keep it in balance. Some athletes see perfectionism as the only way to success, but it isn't the only way and is more properly seen as a tool to be used correctly along the road to their goals. The key for an athlete might be in differentiating and substituting the desire for perfection from an inner desire for more or better. Some describe the inner drive as a hunger or desire. Whether the desire is to win, perfect technique, be dominant or one of the many other things that motivate athletes, a drive that makes the athlete relentlessly pursue their goals is always a part of great success.

Responsibility

Athletes differ in how they understand responsibility and how much they wish to assume responsibility. There are two things about responsibility that we know to be absolutely true. Leaders are always those that take responsibility. In fact, leaders are so strong in this attribute that they can sometimes be found trying to assume responsibility for things that they really did not have any responsibility for or control of to begin with. If a leader does this, a number of undesirable things can be triggered. The leader may become frustrated or angry and blame themselves for problems where they had no control. As they are trying to take responsibility and fix something over which they have little or no control, all sorts of negative emotional problems can be set in motion and attempts at fixing the problem will be quite ineffective. In this situation, the individual or unit who has responsibility and control and those who do not needs to be clearly identified. Only then can the correct entity proceed to use their control to make desired changes. The concept identifying who has the responsibility and control in a situation and that entity accepting that responsibility is crucial to making sense of a situation and making it better.

Now it must be understood that many people are motivated to not accept responsibility for what they do even though it is so damaging to the process of making it better. This resistance to accepting responsibility comes from the emotions they automatically feel in this situation. A small percentage of athletes do not wish to accept responsibility or take credit for reasons such as humility and not wishing to stand out for a number of reasons. Frequently intelligent and sensitive athletes who are nice people fear that they will make less accomplished athletes feel inferior. It is laudable to be concerned about the feelings of others, but this is the wrong solution. It may help these athletes to understand the following:

1. They cannot get inside another persons body and make them feel anything.
2. It is not respecting their own hard work to deny their success.
3. Someone needs to lead the way by example.
4. Each person needs to judge himself by his own standards and not compare himself.
5. If the other person feels bad, they may be able to help them appreciate their own efforts.

When assuming full responsibility for the results of one's own thoughts, feelings and actions, an athlete may judge that their results are inadequate and then feel bad about them. This is a common response, but never to be accepted as a desirable response. If an athlete tried their hardest but still made mistakes and feels bad about them, he needs to understand that this is the wrong response. It is the wrong response because it assumes that we could have done better at the time. This is wrong thinking. Excepting rare circumstances such as we saw in the Olympics where a Korean volleyball team threw a match for a better draw in the next round, athletes always do the best they can at that time. Maybe with the knowledge gained from the execution, or if they had done something different, they might have done better; but that is irrelevant for the competition that has already happened.

After a competition, we can always see what we could have done better. This has been called "Monday morning quarterbacking". All we can ask for, realistically, is to give it our best shot at the time. That's just the way it is and an athlete needs to accept that.

The value of taking appropriate responsibility for our actions cannot be overstated, without it, we cannot take the next step and ask what we did to create the event under consideration. It is much more difficult to take responsibility for our actions and assess them if we feel bad about what we did and think "we should not have done it". If an athlete considers a major goal of every contest as one of obtaining data regarding what works and what does not, they will always be successful. If they won or lost, this is also data. After we have the information concerning how we created what we did, then we can decide what we need to do differently and what training we need to do to make things happen differently in the future. Even if they lost, realizing that they gained important data that can help them compete more effectively the next time can help to neutralize unpleasant emotions. Remember, we are ultimately in control of our feelings and responses unless someone else possesses our body and makes us respond in a certain way independent of our will or actions, an event which I have not witnessed to this point. No matter what happens, if we understand the way to feel good about it the sting is taken out of responsibility making it easier to accept and move forward most effectively.

One final consideration that can be confusing is the role of responsibility in the team setting. Coaches are fond of saying that "there is no I in team" which is supposed to work against individuals being selfish and out for themselves at the cost of the team effort. It is absolutely true that there is no place for selfishness at the cost of the team. However, the team is like a machine which is made up of numerous parts. In any machine, take a car for instance, all the parts need to function as designed for the car to perform as expected. In the news not too long ago there were reports of roll over problems in SUV trucks due to under inflation of tires. Many people liked the softer tires for a softer ride but stability was sacrificed creating significant danger.

In the team context we also want all the components to operate as we wish but frequently coaches do not do a good job of helping players understand the role of individual responsibility in the team effort. The team is a group and group dynamics seen in other places also apply to teams. One important aspect of group dynamics, but almost always undesirable, is the diffusion of responsibility. This is why we often see individuals do undesirable things when in a group or mob, that the same people would not do when on their own. This same diffusion of responsibility combined with anonymity and the thought that they are part of a team effort can interfere with individual members evaluating their own effort sufficiently and identifying what they need to do to operate at their best. The simple response, that is often missed, is for each team member to see them self as a vital link and take full responsibility for developing and executing every part of their job to the highest level possible. It is not unusual for an athlete to wish to avoid responsibility when things do not go well. The goal of this attitude is to avoid guilt or shame regarding their execution based on anonymity and diffusion of responsibility. However, not taking responsibility for what they did makes them helpless to review the cause and effect of their actions which provides the basis to create change.

Chapter 4

ESSENTIAL CONCEPTS:
KEY OPERATIVE KNOWLEDGE

Introduction

Key Operative Knowledge concerns not only useful ways to think about concepts integral to performance in sports, but also specific things the athlete needs to do. Recall the concept that power is the ability to take action. It is not enough to understand the concepts that are key to creating the best performance, it is necessary to take different action if you want a different outcome. In my office, once the athlete and I have decided what is holding their performance down and what they need to do differently, I then have them write down what they are going to do differently and when they are going to do it. That will be their assignment and the next meeting we have the specifics of what they were supposed to do and when they intended to do it to compare with their actions. As with most of the things we discuss in this book it is important to create specific behavioral strategies of what will be done, when they will do it and how many repetitions they will execute so you have specific data to evaluate the strategy in light of results. There are many names for this process in the psychology of creating change. One strategy is called

TOTE which stands for test, operate, test and exit. This means test the situation to see what you have, operate the strategy that is supposed to create the intended change and test the situation again to see if the strategy had the desired effect. If the strategy got the intended response, then you know what works and you may decide to continue with the same strategy. If you did not get the intended change when you test it, you then can amend the strategy as you wish, operate it again and then test again to see if you got the response you wish.

The concept of 'successive approximations' may come into play here. This concept is discussed more completely in the section on short term goals but briefly, at times when you wish to achieve a goal it is useful to break the goal down to components and then achieve the goal one component at a time. You start with the most basic component and after it is achieved go to the next one adding the components until you are executing the goal behavior. For example, if you wanted your kid to be at school and in their classroom ready to learn at first period you would start with making sure the most basic component was either in place or have a strategy developed to put it in place. Each situation is different to some extent but the progression might be, get a good night sleep, wake up at the right time, eat the right breakfast, get dressed at the right time, gather materials needed for school, take materials when leaving for school at the right time and get to class in time for it to start. This model can be applied to almost any desired change in human behavior and is often combined with the TOTE process to evaluate and review something that you would like to change, see where things went wrong and identify an alternative behavior or even a short term goal to introduce at that point.

SelfTalk

We all talk to ourselves in our own mind almost constantly, whether we know it or not. We talk about things we encounter, what we think, what we feel, who we are, what we are capable of doing and what we expect to happen. The things we tell ourselves can have a huge impact on all aspects of our life, in the present and in the future. For example, if a tennis player tells himself that an opponent is going to be really hard to beat and focuses on how difficult it will be to compete; the body will ingeniously, at an unconscious level, find ways to make the match more difficult. If the player approaches the same match with a optimistic attitude and competition procedures designed to create his best, he will bring his best game regardless of the competition.

Research has shown that we tend to automatically live out whatever we say to ourselves, whether it is good or bad. Desirable self talk should be positive and focus on what we want to occur. The rule to follow is that we want to talk to ourselves about only what we want the situation to be or what we want to happen. This is not to say that changing our thoughts will change the outward reality, but changing out thoughts will change how we function and respond to the outside world which creates a different outward reality. For example, many times we have seen a golfer who seems to always have problems with hazards. Even though he aims away, the ball seems to always find it's way back to the hazard. He may be thinking to himself "don't hit it in the hazard" but all his unconscious mind hears is hazard and targets the hazard. What he needs to do is think only of what he wants and that is what his unconscious mind will tend to produce. So alternately, he would need to think, I am going to hit it there, wherever he wants it to be and to some extent his body will automatically make that happen. The desired results are not guaranteed, but the general tendency will be to move in the desired direction. This procedure, combined with other procedures, mount up to create a higher likelihood of the desired result.

A good exercise is to try to be aware of what you say to yourself in any situation of interest and make a list over time of what you find yourself saying silently in your mind. Then review the list and see if anything you do not want is identified. Next, go over the list and substitute the description of what you do want for that of what you do not want. A runner might find himself thinking "I'm slow out of the blocks" and decide to say "I'm getting faster out of the blocks". Basically, it can be said that any thoughts or things we say to our self to create optimism and describe a positive direction for events, will positively affect the IPS and subtly influence events in the desired direction.

One must also be wary of negative self talk masquerading as positive. This can be found in any statements about what you do not want, such as "Don't be nervous", or "I don't want to hit it in the woods." Better choices would be "I'm going to feel great today", or "Today I am feeling more comfortable and confident." Try to use the principle of self talk in a proactive manner where instead of focusing on avoiding a problem, you decide just how you want to feel or how you want things to go and tell yourself that what you have decided you want to happen will happen. The execution part of the mind tends to not hear the "don't or not" so if an athlete tells them self "don't hit it in the woods or don't be nervous", all the mind hears is hit it in the woods or nervous, and says "ok here it is, you asked for it and you got it."

An example of proactive self talk could be "All of my good work is beginning to pay off and my putting is getting dialed in" or simply "I feel great today and this is going to be easy." Of course, things don't magically appear just because you say they will. It just seems like magic, because speaking correctly to your self and putting the right thoughts into your mind can have an enormous impact to move events in the desired direction. A parent of a girl I was training once told me that another parent asked him "how can she come off the bench and immediately play at that high level?" I told him the simple answer for the parent is, "she knows how to do it." A group exercise I often do consists of a player holding her arm out and resisting another player pulling it down. In one trial another player whispers positive thoughts to them and this is followed by the player whispering negative thoughts. Although the player can resist well in the positive thought condition, when they hear the negative thoughts they become weaker and their arm will practically collapse. Most people have no clue how powerful their mind is in creating the reality they experience.

Beliefs and Expectations

Beliefs and Expectations can determine outcome, including failure and success. Just like the things we say to ourselves, the things we believe to be true or expect to happen will seem to manifest themselves automatically. In general psychology, this process is called "the self fulfilling prophesy". In medicine the same process is called the "placebo effect". Doctors used to see the placebo effect as a confounding irritant but have more recently incorporated it into standard medical care. It has been known for years that whatever a person believes will happen, even at an unconscious level, will tend to happen automatically. At times, luck has been wrongly believed to be the cause of things happening to a person, whether good or bad; but the process of self fulfilling prophecy is usually the cause.

Many times, we have observed athletes underperform in a contest and found out later that they did not believe they could be effective in the situation and did not expect a positive outcome. That small bit of doubt can easily be magnified a hundred times. The important message here is that we can influence the future while it is being created by what we believe to be true and expect to happen. And once again, this happens outside our awareness.

There is an old saying that applies here that I use all the time; "It is better to aim high because if you miss, you will miss high, than to aim low and hit what you are aiming at." Athletes commonly have asked, "What if I expect to play real well or win and it doesn't happen, won't I be disappointed?" The answer is "Sure you will be disappointed! But disappointment is an absolutely unavoidable fact of life. We need to learn to handle it in a productive way." The key here is that by believing and expecting the positive we will become most effective in moving toward what we want, and this is our goal. If fear of failure is so prominent that we do not try our best because we might not achieve what we want, then we have a problem that will hurt us in every aspect of life. This must be addressed at the earliest possible time. We will always make mistakes if we are pushing the frontier of our ability. The key is to accept mistakes and learn how to use the information generated by mistakes to help us move on as rapidly and powerfully as possible.

Mental Routines

Mental routines (also called pre-performance rituals) are a sequence of actions the athlete takes in the same sequence just before they initiate execution. This could be a pre-hitting routine for a batter, or pre-serve or pre-receiving routine for a tennis player. Golfers have used pre-shot routines for many years. I once had a Division One golfer who was ranked #1 nationally at the time come to me just to get advice on components of his pre-shot routine. The purpose of the routine is to help the athlete create more consistent high level performance. A couple of examples might help here. One figure skater would always check her boot-laces the last thing before she went out to skate her performance. She had no reason to believe her laces were not correct, but the check was more part of the process of locking her mind into the focus she had decided was best to execute at the highest level, that is, in her IPS. Another figure skater who has won several gold medals would always "high five" his coach the last thing before he went out to start his program as part of his pre-performance routine or ritual. You may have observed basketball players who always bounce the ball a certain number of times before taking a free throw. Wade Boggs, the great baseball player, had an elaborate pre-performance routine that included arriving at the field at a certain time and doing several things in the same way before the beginning of every game. His teammates used to say they could "set their watch by the time he took the field for batting practice." Many of the things athletes have done which have been called superstitions, although they would seem to have no direct impact on execution, have been helpful because they were part of a routine that set or kept in motion a series of events, including thoughts and feelings, that would help get them into the IPS prior to the actual performance.

This has always seemed a mysterious process, probably the reason some of these behaviors have been label "superstitions" over the years. However, understanding the process takes the mystery out and also provides the formula for success. Once the IPS for the given athlete is discovered and the processes creating the desired beliefs, feelings, focus, expectations, beliefs and energy level have been identified, a pre execution routine can be constructed. When this routine is followed before every event whether it is hitting, racing or whatever, the athlete will predictably go into the IPS and create the highest level of execution he has developed the capability of creating at the time. Repeating this routine over time makes it easier to obtain the desired result and is observed as consistency.

Using Goals

In the past, many athletes have hated setting goals because they felt goals increased pressure to perform and also felt that goals provided a criteria making it easier to judge them to be a failure if the goals weren't reached. These concerns reflect undesirable things that have happened resulting from improper ways of thinking about and using goals. However, if goals are used properly, these negative results do not manifest. Using goals properly is an essential part of every athlete becoming their best. Even people who do not understand an effective goal setting process or even say they hate goals, use goals whether they acknowledge it or not because without some type of goal you have chaos and less goal directed behavior.

One description of goals I like is "Goals are like stars to the ancient mariners. We can use them to steer our course even though we may never reach them". This would refer to large global goals such as being an Olympian or setting a significant record. On the other hand, the path to the chance to obtain the large long term goals is to set short term process goals that direct our behavior and create reinforcement of continued activity along the path. Goal setting and proper methods for helping students obtain goals is an essential part of teacher education that requires significant work at the university level to master. Although a complete mastery of this topic is beyond the scope of our discussion here, we can achieve an understanding of the goal setting and attainment process that will help you oversee and evaluate this essential part of your athlete's sport experience.

Understanding and Using Long Term Goals

Long-term goals give us direction, purpose and focus. We may reach our long term goals, such as win an Olympic championship, or we might not, but good goal directed behavior is an essential part of any meaningful attempt to reach them. Long-term goals range from what one would like to achieve in the next few months or years, such as making it to playoffs, to longer range goals such as winning an Olympic medal. Although many dream of having an Olympic spot or a career in professional sports, few are chosen. Many children have these dreams and that is fine because dreams are a big part of the childhood sport experience. It is fine to let them dream and go for it to the best of their ability so they can see what they can do. It is important that parents provide the support that children need without pushing. This confusing situation is reviewed in another section of this book. If the time comes where the child has reached a level where they cannot be competitive any longer, and for most that time comes prior to making it to the Olympics or professional level, then the best response to the situation can be determined by realistically looking at the current situation and will usually include an appreciation for what has been done.

A gifted tennis player recently told me that she intended to compete at the professional level until she had achieved as much as possible and then go full time into teaching. Although it is not necessary to know how far they can go or what they will do when they have achieved all they can, my message is to let children dream and pursue their goals to the extent of their ability. If they do not reach the level they sought and if their career has been handled properly, they have a career of wonderful experiences to look back on which forms an excellent template upon which to pursue other things they seek. Many employment recruiters aggressively seek collegiate athletes because they realize that athletes successful at that level have an established ability to marshal their abilities in pursuit of a goal.

In summary, the two major functions of long term goals are to provide direction and motivation. Once the long term goal is identified in terms of what the athlete wants to achieve, the next logical step is to determine what needs to be done to get there. Working backward from the long term goal leads to identification of the steps that need to be taken in the process. These steps are the short term goals. The confusing topic of motivation is discussed in another section of the book. At this point, let it be said that the child having dreams and pursuing them with joy and excitement is also one of the most valuable templates for pursuing their goals later in life and needs to be respected and nurtured appropriately.

Medium range goals can be thought of as short term/long term goals as they have elements of both. Medium range goals, like competing at one's best in a competition, making a certain score or accomplishing some other objective such as getting a first serve in, can be used for direction like a long term goal but also provide a measure of the current level of performance and reinforcement of effort like a short term goal. Medium range goals can also include emotional goals such as being comfortable in the tee box for a golfer, getting rid of undesirable mind/body experiences such as the "yips" which usually are seen in putting or short shots and execution processes such as straightening out a drive or handling the threat of hazards effectively.

Understanding and Using Short Term Goals

Short term goals can and should be broken down to the smallest relevant unit and built upon from there. The concept of "successive approximations" again comes into play here. All execution is built of components. Successive approximations is the processes where you start with the first or smallest component of the end execution goal and step by step build ability with the components until all the components of the end execution goal are at the level that is desired. At that point the end execution goal is achieved.

For example, take a football player who needed to run a 6 minute mile to gain entrance to the team but was very overweight and had never run at all. The first goal might be to get him some running shoes. The next goal could be for him to start way before the season and, after being cleared by a doctor, run once a day until he was tired and felt like stopping. By stopping when he got tired, running would not become a task he wished to avoid. Because running is not made negative, he would be more likely to continue running and eventually, he would get in better condition and be able to run faster. At this level of developing the abilities necessary to be on the team, the athlete should be encouraged to feel a sense of accomplishment and satisfaction for just working at it. It is very important to monitor the athlete's goals and responses to their work outs to make sure they do not take on too much too soon and become discouraged or injured.

What sometimes seems a mystery with regard to what needs to be done to improve performance at the optimal rate can become clearer by breaking the task demands of the situation down into components. Then using the principle of successive approximations specific short term goals can be identified that start from the simplest goal and gradually increased in difficulty while rewarding the attainment of each approximation of the final goal in the appropriate way to maintain motivation. If the goal is too difficult resulting in failure, then it should be cut back to a simpler approximation, that is, an obtainable goal and then increased incrementally as the athlete has success until the ultimate goal has been achieved. A general rule of goal setting that make this process easier and most productive is that goals should be specific, measurable and contain a time factor.

An example of a poorly stated short term goal in golf would be to have a better drive in golf. A better example of short term goals to create a better drive in golf would be to first take a proper stance every time. Once a proper stance is always created, the next goal might be the proper grip, every time. The next short term goal might be a proper take away. After a proper takeaway is consistent, then a proper swing, including being on plane, proper body coordination and the rest of correct technique all the way to the correct follow through might be the final piece. Once all the pieces of a good drive are built, the entire sequence should be practiced until it is consistent. This might be an over simplification, but the point is to break the desired behavior down to the smallest components that are reasonable and master each piece until the final skill is developed. This process is by definition successive approximations. With completion of each component, the athlete should be encouraged to feel good about developing each piece to the desired level. This is known as "reinforcement" and it will support positive feelings, positive view of oneself and encourage the athlete to achieve more.

Another example could be the task of a receiver in football. The receiver needs to start at the right time, run their route correctly, possibly throw a good fake, be aware of the ball, catch the ball with good concentration and good technique, lock the ball in so it cannot be dislodged by the defense and then try to get some yardage. Each task is a short term goal that needs to be practiced and brought to an appropriate level of consistently. Even if the ball was knocked loose by the defense, the receiver should be encouraged to feel good about what they did right and then focus on the short term goal of holding on to the ball once they have it. Frequently, a receiver will look at the total sequence and feel bad because they did not hold on to it. A more effective way to look at it is to feel good about the things done right; then isolate and practice the part of locking the ball safely into their grip until that part is executed at the desired level.

The old adage of "no pain, no gain" needs to be understood and handled properly. It is true that a well conditioned athlete will frequently push workouts to the point they feel some muscle fatigue that could be considered a type of pain. This type of working hard is necessary in the competitive environment; however, there are types of physical and psychological pain that should never be ignored and the workout continued. It can be very difficult to know when to stop and when to continue. Athletes have been struggling with this question forever and the answers are not clear cut. As a parent, you must make sure this question is being answered correctly for your child. The best advice I can give is gather enough information from the coach, trainers and doctors to feel that you and your child understand some guidelines and continue to monitor the situation as needed.

In addition to creating the performance that is desired short-term goals should not be forgotten as a tremendously valuable source of reinforcement and motivation. Encouraging short-term goals for every practice, with appropriate degrees of difficulty, provides clear direction and the feeling of mastery and feeling of success in achieving them. When you set out to achieve a goal and you do not make it, you are provided an opportunity to evaluate your training process, including your method for achieving the goal or possibly the appropriateness of the goal itself. When evaluating a goal, you can ask several questions:

1. Was the goal appropriately achievable? If not, change it.
2. Was the method to achieve the goal the right method?
3. Was the time period long enough to permit achievement of the goal?

It should be expected that you will constantly be reviewing the process of successive approximations and adjusting the process to be more efficient. This helps you become more effective in practice and additionally, creates the same type of situation presented by competition where you are attempting to achieve certain goals and want to deal with the process of attaining them as effectively as possible.

There is quite a bit of knowledge regarding the sport, the stage of training, and athlete variables that goes into setting the appropriate direction of short, medium and long-term goals. The person most capable of setting these goals in serious youth sports programs is the coach. As a parent, it is important that you discuss goals and your perceptions with the coach so you will all be on the same page and so you will be able to effectively monitor the situation. Assuming you have a qualified coach, you must respect their experience and guidance, but continue to monitor the situation. There are coaches who, for one reason or another, do not provide an environment with a goal progression that is right for your child. It may be possible that the goals of the particular program might not be what your child needs. For example, the program may be a competitive program where your child just beginning the sport may profit more from a program that emphasizes participation. If you have concerns or questions, I suggest that you discuss it with the coach. If you still are not satisfied, you may want to consult other sources of information and possibly even obtain a consultation from a sport psychologist.

As with other situations in this environment you face, it is important to use well considered judgment here to find the right level of oversight and intervention to exercise. The parent becoming too intrusive and over involved can create additional workload and distraction that can be harmful to both the child and sport program. On the other hand, not being involved enough can allow your child to be in an inappropriate environment which can also be harmful in many ways including wasted time, slow development and discouragement so getting it right is pretty important for an optimal sport experience. The concept of parental involvement, communication, and making choices is central to the sport experience of a child and is discussed in several other places in this book.

Chapter 5
MENTAL SKILLS

Introduction

In addition to the information about the best way to think and suggestions for effective mental procedures to execute that are contained in Essential Concepts, there are two major elements in the Mental Training Program that comprise what I refer to as Mental Skills, Mental Focusing Skills and Mental Imagery Skills. This area of knowledge and techniques is the most complicated and difficult to gain from a book at an optimal level. Some valuable information can be obtained from a book but developing effective mental focusing skills and proper use of them is a very technique intensive process. In addition, there are almost infinite variations to the imagery technique which can be used for specific goals and proper choice of technique components and modifications of imagery technique to make the process effective is a very technical endeavor. Some information is better than none but the services of a qualified sport psychologist is irreplaceable if the goal is to create optimal level of use of this area of mental training. Goals in this area can take awhile to develop due to the complexity of the material, but it is also true that one or two sessions may be all that is needed to get the athlete on the right track.

Mental Focusing Skills

Mental Focusing Skill training teaches athletes how to concentrate so they can focus their mind and body more completely, more accurately for the task demands of the situation and at the correct level of intensity. Mental Focusing Skills are roughly divided into two subtypes. One type is mind/body focusing skills that allow the athlete to sense the level of arousal in their mind and body and be able to adjust it to the IPS. The other type is purely mental and is used to increase the power of concentration enabling the athlete to block out distractions and isolate the focus of attention more completely for sport demands, such as concentrating to catch a pass with defenders closing in, or to change and reprogram habits more easily.

Using the mind/body focusing skills, athletes are able to become aware of the tension level in isolated areas of their body, as well as a general level of arousal between the extremes of being very highly energized or anxious and being totally relaxed. The ability is then developed to adjust the level of energy in any part of the body or the overall level of arousal at will.

Long ago one of the first uses of sport psychology was to teach athletes who were experiencing performance anxiety to relax. When this was done, these athletes moved more into their IPS and were then able to execute more effectively as a result. Early sport psychologists and coaches, with limited knowledge, then concluded that relaxation was good for everyone. As a result, when they relaxed athletes who did not need it, those athletes then went below their IPS and did worse. This was certainly harmful to those athletes and the field of sport psychology got a black eye and bad reputation early on for being ineffective. After the situation was better understood, this practice was corrected. Some athletes find value in using relaxation techniques before and during a competition and some do not. This highlights the necessity for performing an individual assessment of task demands and specific athlete needs before doing anything.

Although relaxation skills are not the right technique to use for every athlete before a contest, they are still correctly used as a training technique in the general development of mental skills for most athletes. One of the major mental focusing skills I teach as part of the mental training program is called Progressive Deep Muscle Relaxation (PDMR). With golfers, I have found that if I do not start with PDMR, I usually have to go back to it later. This is because the game of golf puts a premium on sensing subtle levels and changes in the tension of the body. PDMR is the best training technique for the ability to adjust tension level to the IPS. One professional golfer found, after training in PDMR, that he could sense a specific line of tension from his shoulder to his left wrist that was present every time his swing went off in a specific way. From the PDMR training, he was able not only to gain this additional information; but also able to relax the tension and his swing would come back, every time.

PDMR was first introduced by Herbert Benson, M.D., a cardiologist, as a technique to counter the stress response, which is usually a cardiovascular risk factor, with the relaxation response triggered by PDMR. Examples of this technique and instructions can be found in his book. In the past I have created recordings of the exercise, which people love, and will probably do so again if there is sufficient demand. Some authors in sport psychology have stated that PDMR is probably the best mental focusing technique to start with in training because it is so easy to do and has such wide utility to reduce anxiety, reduce stress, develop greater awareness of the mind/body state and as a first stage training procedure in the general development of mental skills.

While PDMR is a physically based mind/body exercise, the other main class of mental focusing skills consists of purely mentally based techniques. These skills involve focusing the mind and attention in ways similar to meditation or self-hypnosis where the attention is progressively focused on one thing so it can be used more powerfully for many different goals. This kind of focusing can be compared to asking a class of students to focus only on a light switch. In a normally lighted room, they could see the light switch but could also be easily distracted by the other things they could also see in their field of vision. However, in a dark room where a flash light was focused only on the light switch and everything else was in darkness, it would be much easier to focus only on the light switch. The primary role of mentally based mental focusing techniques is to teach the athletes to create this type of powerful focus which makes it much easier to program or reprogram the mind for the desired operations. This powerful focusing ability allows the athlete to access the part of the mind where habitual ways of thinking, feeling and acting are stored as programs and reprogram themselves in any way desired.

Mental Focusing training is also used to adjust the type of general mental focus or thinking athletes engage in at any specific time. The ability to choose the type of perception used to make the choices of right or left brain thinking, to be applied at specific times, has important implications for training and competition. Interestingly, some children diagnosed with attention deficit hyperactivity disorder (ADHD) have reported increases in their ability to focus on schoolwork after participating in Mental Training. Unfortunately, learning mental focusing skills, like meditation, is dependent on subtle technique choices and although quite easy to learn with a mental coach, it can be quite difficult to learn without one.

Mental Imagery Skills

Mental Imagery Skill Training teaches an athlete the techniques used to manipulate mental pictures and other sensory perceptions after the mind has been focused. Once again, because the mind operates using specific mental mechanics, use of correctly matching mental technique can dramatically increase effectiveness. Good intention and desire is great, but understanding the mental mechanics by which the mind operates can have an enormous impact upon the productivity of Mental Imagery practice. Once again, correct goal and technique choices are very instrumental to success with mental imagery work and it is very difficult to learn the many subtleties important to use it effectively without coaching from a highly qualified mental coach who specializes in this type of thing. Several times I have had athletes come to me and say "the coach has told me to use mental imagery, but I just keep getting worse." In those cases I have told the athletes "stop doing it." Invariably, I have found that the technique they were using was wrong. Once I coached them on the right way to do it, they started getting good results.

Mental Imagery used with Mental Focusing can be used to program the mind to achieve a wide range of goals which include, but are not limited to, the following:

Achieve the correct IPS

Automatically feel desirable feelings and think desirable thoughts at a specific time

Groove in specific technique

Eliminate undesirable technique and bad habits

Build and groove pre-performance routines that create the IPS

Create a trigger to instantly go into a desired focus or emotional state

Create a trigger to instantly enter the IPS or access the Zone when desired

More effectively mentally rehearse a competition, such as a round of golf, to more automatically play as desired in the competition.

In summary, mental imagery skills are the mental processes employed after the mind has been focused appropriately to attain many of the goals of sport psychology. Beginning with a deep mental focus makes it easier to concentrate fully on one thing, creates more access to the majority of athlete resources at the physical and mental level and makes it easier to reprogram the mind to operate as desired in the future. However, use of mental imagery in a standard mental level of focus can also have mental training value. Both modes of using mental imagery have a place in the skill set of an athlete. Mental imagery, as discussed here, includes not only pictures in your mind but also mental representations of what you want to feel (kinesthetic imagery), hear (auditory imagery) and smell (olfactory imagery). At times, it is most useful to isolate one representation system, such as kinesthetic, where a golfer may want to both feel totally confident on the first tee and be able to create the feel of an excellent tee shot. At other times, it creates a more powerful mental training effect to include more of the representation systems of visual, auditory, kinesthetic and olfactory systems. A preprogramming for success example of this would be when an athlete is imagining himself seeing, feeling, believing, and acting as desired in an future event as a strategy to program himself to automatically go into the desired focus and responses during the actual event.

Although mental focusing skills provide a fertile basis to use mental imagery skills for a variety of practice goals, they also have a place in performance. If, for example, a golfer tends to feel uncomfortable in the tee box, they can use mental focusing skills to get to the right level of relaxation/energy desired and then use mental imagery skills to program themselves to automatically feel comfortable, confident of success and create the swing they want. In another example, I was working with a football team teaching them the Essential Concepts program to generally increase their performance. As usual, the team was increasing the quality of their performance every game, but one lineman was vomiting before each game. The player needed only to be told how to use his mental skills to reduce the level of his physiological arousal and he was able to immediately stop vomiting which made him more comfortable. Incidentally, the already outstanding lineman was able to increase his effectiveness because he felt better and was able to keep the pregame meal in his body for energy.

Once again, mental skills are very difficult to learn from a book, but knowledge gained from a book can put an athlete much further ahead than not having any at all. Some general benefits can be derived from using information in books; but alleviation of tenacious problems or maximum results are unlikely to be gained without mental coaching. Remember, just as sport psychologists vary widely in their training, knowledge and expertise, books also vary widely in the accuracy and value of their information so it is imperative for you to carefully evaluate the sources of information you use. Mental Skills training is the most technically complex component of mental training and high level assistance in this area is the most difficult to obtain so it may be necessary to interview numerous providers before you find one qualified in this area of expertise.

Chapter 6

MOTIVATION

Introduction

While at a game recently with a team, I ran into a father who asked me if I got the team motivated. I said no and he looked confused. I told him that my role was not to motivate them, but to give them mental skills they could use to play more effectively. When people think of sport psychology and it's link to success in sports, the first and often only thing they often think about is motivation. Although motivation is an important part of the equation for success, it is not the sole factor. You might say it is a necessity, but not the only core element sufficient for success. Necessity is a key word here though because in my over 35 years of working with the highest level athletes in the world, the one thing that always was there at a high level athlete was motivation. An athlete will never get anywhere close to realizing their potential without a significant, and usually massive, amount of motivation. The reason is that the things required to be great in a sport require significant amounts of work in addition to everything else. Henry Ford knew this as he was once heard to say, "I'll take one man with complete commitment to 100 men with just interest."

It will serve you greatly to have a basic understanding of the motivation of your child if you want to provide them the greatest opportunity for success. Children have different sources of motivation in sports and they are not all the same regarding the relative value of one motivation versus another. Although you may have been an athlete in the same sport, it would be a mistake to assume that your child would be motivated for the same reason you were. The chance for a difference in motivation increases with a difference in sex and a change in sport. Understanding what is important about the sport to your child is a giant step towards determining how you can be most helpful. All of the types of motivations I will describe can have a positive effect or be misused to the detriment of the child.

Motivation has been defined in many ways, but is basically the desire to act to gain a reward. This is what drives all people, the carrot and the whip. We try to get the carrot and avoid the whip. The function of a reward such as the carrot is to increase the tendency of the athlete to demonstrate goal directed behavior which is intended to result in obtaining the reward. The function of the whip or other punishment is to decrease the frequency of the behavior that produces undesirable results.

Different athletes see different things as rewards and punishments. It is important to know what your child likes about the sport so that the correct carrot can be used. Although the whip, in metaphor or literally, has been used in the past by some coaches and parents with some success, I generally discourage any type of negative input from coaches and parents. Sometimes, punishments such as running laps if the athlete is late or demonstrates lack of effort have been successfully used by coaches, but I prefer a more creative approach which provides rewards for desired behavior. There are an overwhelming number of negative things associated with punishment as a motivation. Rewarding desirable actions with praise or positive feelings and punishing undesirable actions with negative input is called 'differential reinforcement' and has some limited value. However, you may wish to remember the results of a study where subjects were asked to perform a difficult task. Where subjects were given positive reinforcement and support during the task, 80% finished the task in the allotted time, but when subjects were provided negative and critical input, only 20% finished the task. Be very careful with negative input and punishment for actions that you wish to reduce and support your athlete with positive attitudes and emotions as much as possible.

There are two general classes of motivation that you may be familiar with to some extent. These general classes of motivation are Internal and External motivation. These are sometimes also called Intrinsic and Extrinsic motivation.

External Motivation
External or extrinsic motivation refers to any situation where the motivational drive to take action or achieve results comes from some place or someone other than the athlete personally. External motivation could be praise for achievement, trophies, money, appreciation, respect from peers, acknowledgement by the media, a ranking or positive supportive statements from parents to name a few.

Internal Motivation
Internal motivation is the condition where the rewards for activity such as training or achievement are experienced within the athlete.

Generally, this involves a thought or feeling generated within the athlete's mind. Examples include feeling good about simply making a shot or winning an entire competition. A healthy example from training might be the athlete feeling good about completing a hard work out or achieving some other short term goal. Just showing up regularly or having a positive thought or feeling about one's self can create a spark of internal motivation. As will be discussed later, many athletes derive internal motivation from a variety of sources that are not commonly considered. For example, just participating in a sport they feel is unique and sets them apart from their peers is a motivation for some. Some of this motivation can be seen in the Extreme or X-game sports. However, the adrenalin rush is also a common intrinsic reward in these sports.

There are many different types of motivation which will be discussed later in greater detail. However, it is important to understand what a positive motivator or reward can be. The simple answer is that it can be anything that makes the athlete experience a positive feeling. When an athlete experiences something positive as a result of something they did, the likelihood of doing that same thing again is increased. This is the definition of positive reinforcement and is the basis of motivation. This is an important concept because the same things are not motivators for all people. One child might respond extremely well to praise and feel very good about himself, but praise in general or from a different coach, parent or other person might not mean as much to another child. The reinforcement value of a reward depends on what the athlete values.

It is generally thought that internal motivation is the healthiest, most effective, and lasts the longest because it is much more under the athlete's control. An internally motivated athlete is less dependent on others or on unreliable external sources of reward. Being dependent on outside sources for good feelings or other rewards for a job well accomplished makes the athlete somewhat vulnerable to the whims of others. For example, if an athlete must win a tennis match in order to feel good about the effort, then the athlete's feelings about himself would be dependent on things over which there was not complete control. Outside factors such as winning the game, line calls, etc. can affect his feeling of well-being and impact his play. An internal reward based on the athlete's performance in terms of effort is much more under the athlete's control. The reward for a great effort or great play could be obtained internally, regardless of the play of the other competitor or the outcome of the match. Some sources of rewards tend to be more external or internally based.

The results of one study found that when external motivation was applied to an athlete who was known to be internally motivated, the amount of internal motivation actually decreased over time. Beware of depressing the internal motivation of your athlete by applying excessive external motivation. This is something to keep your eye on.

On the other hand, a skater who was very talented said she wanted to master a certain jump, but was having a hard time completing it. Because of the lack of success, her effort and frequency of attempts had obviously decreased. Her mother, in a fit of desperation, told her she would give her a dollar for every one of these jumps she could make in a row. The skater attacked the jump with renewed enthusiasm and did more of the jumps than she had done in the entire last week. Now this apparent bribery, with a seemingly unrelated external reward, is usually the very thing that most sport psychologists counsel parents and coaches not to do. But in this situation, it worked. It was the spark that enabled the athlete to break out of her pattern and realize she could do more than she believed. She continued to attack this jump more effectively without further monetary reward although she did attempt to convince her mother that the money should keep flowing. In this instance, we then got the athlete focused back on experiencing internal satisfaction from her effort, and the success that resulted, and continued from there with the internal motivation exclusively.

Motivation Types and Needs

As previously mentioned, rewards and the motivation which they fuel, are not the same for all individuals. A number of the main types of rewards that different athletes are motivated to achieve are explained in this section. Many of these categories of rewards or sources of motivation have several names and vary in internal and external components. As you read about them and evaluate the degree of relevance they have for your athlete, you may be able to gain valuable understanding of why your child athlete engages in his/her activities.

Winning

Winning the contest is a common reward for the work put into a sport with which we are the most familiar. Within the category of winning, there may be a variety of internal as well as external rewards depending on the orientation of the athlete. The trophy, ranking and appreciation from others are external rewards but the satisfaction for the achievement is internally focused.

Ability Orientation

Ability Orientation is the name given to the motivation the athlete feels by attributing significant ability to himself. Although one may be motivated by other rewards also, an athlete high in ability orientation is rewarded by feeling good because they consider themselves to have significant ability in the particular sport. Their ability to attribute these feelings or perceptions to themselves will be obviously dependent on their success, according to their standard. The important point here is that the experience of feeling that they have high ability for the sport is the reward.

Mastery of Sport

Mastery of the sport or skill is another motivational force for many athletes. This athlete will be distinguished by feeling good that they mastered a challenging task. This is a strong motivation and a great many athletes are driven for this reason. For an athlete who wants to achieve at a high level, this motivation is very valuable as it rewards the hard work and time spent on developing skills. This skill perfecting activity makes available short-term goal rewards that help keep the athlete positive, motivated, and focused.

Mastery of An Opponent or Motivation for Power

Mastery of an opponent, also known as a motivation for power, is another motivation important to some athletes. This motivation often found in sports like boxing and wrestling, can also be found in any other individual or team sport where the athlete's intention is focused on defeating the opponent. This can be a very healthy motivation couched in the form of competitiveness. However, if the athlete demonstrates pleasure in the misfortune or injury of others, there is good reason to investigate the meaning of the athlete's motivation.

Adventure

Adventure is another motivation for some athletes. Adventure is defined here as taking on a risky or possibly dangerous challenge. It is also defined as a quality of a sport that is described as exciting or remarkable. Of course, this has a lot to do with what is defined by the individual as adventure and can be found in team sports such as football, as well as the typical extreme sports such as kayaking, snowboarding, rock climbing, skateboarding and extreme skiing. Adventure is often present during the learning of a sport, in addition to the sports where adventure is the primary motivation. Some athletes enjoy the challenge of adventure, but most report the intensity as a very important factor to them. The experience of intensity carries a strong psycho-physiological reward component. This is why athletes who do one intense sport may also enjoy other sports which have the same intensity component.

Social Recognition

Social recognition and approval is a motivation that many athletes experience. In fact, many athletes who rise to high levels openly use the adoration of fans as a reward and motivation to keep working hard. Many musical performers or actors also report this type of motivation and say they crave it and miss it when they no longer perform or compete. Social recognition from sports can provide the athlete resources that become rewards at many levels. Recognition for either participating or success can have a legitimate positive effect on an athlete's self esteem. In some cases, this can be reason enough to encourage children into a sport that is right for them so they can experience this type of reward.

Physical Conditioning

Some individuals are motivated to engage in a sport primarily to gain the physical conditioning that results. Although this is a laudable goal, it can be difficult to maintain motivation for this reason alone. To make it easiest to continue in the sport for conditioning or health, other enjoyable goals or components can be added to the sport activity. An example that comes to mind is that many runners who run to be fit find it easier to continue running when they do it with other people or run with a musical device.

Peer Group Involvement

Another source of motivation to be in and do well in sports is the natural desire for group membership. In less clinical terms, humans are social beings and many desirable results come from being part of a team striving for some goal. Many athletes, particularly at the younger ages, experience a very healthy peer group motivation to be involved in sports. In group sports, the child gets to experience camaraderie and develop the many social skills learned from being in a group. Some of the social rewards discussed earlier are present, but the feeling of belonging and participating in a joint effort is primary in this category and a good reason for a child to be in a sport.

This situation actually mirrors the situation that many adults find themselves in at work or other social settings. In teams with a healthy environment, social and emotional skills that children will need later are learned, refined and improved. In the business world, the ability to work well with others as part of a team is highly valued and rewarded.

Avoidance of Failure

In playing the sport, motivation to avoid failure may surface. Avoiding failure is usually a poor and short-lived motivator. Motivation by trying to avoid making mistakes has some logical and real basis. However, if the athlete focuses too much on not committing errors or achieving undesirable results, serious impediments to performance will develop. It seems logical not to want to make mistakes; but the key in simple terms is to only use the desire not to fail to encourage desired behavior. This motivation, if used in a positive way can contribute to our effort to be precise and effective. Some athletes say this is an important source of motivation for them to train and compete hard. However, when this motivation is too high athletes create many undesirable behaviors such as playing safe and not taking risks causing the effort and result to be less than it could have been. Beyond the limited appropriate use of this motivation, athletes usually perform best when totally focusing on what is needed to get the job done and positive rewards.

Matching Motivation to Child

If you observe the sport choices of athletes, you will find that although many will participate in several different sports for a change, a large number of athletes will focus on one as their primary sport. However, motivation and the interest of the child athlete can change over time, especially with young athletes. There is a trend toward overspecialization too early in child athletics. There are dangers in this approach that can be researched in greater detail in other publications.

After enjoying success and fun in one sport and many dollars invested, a child can lose interest and quit altogether. This can be confusing and extremely frustrating to the parents, coach, instructor or other team members. However, it is important to try and understand why or how the disinterest developed. At one time, a disturbing situation was noticed where significant numbers of talented child athletes were found to be quitting sports in which they excelled. Research was then conducted to determine why athletes with promising capabilities were quitting their sport. A partial list of reasons stated by children for quitting a sport are:

1. No longer fun, either from too much parental or coach pressure.
2. Too many other demands on the child.
3. The child wants to work instead.
4. Body shape and coordination changes impacting the sport become frustrating.
5. Other children catch up in skill and physical attributes affecting the competition.
6. School grades and social life are compromised.
7. They get bored with the sport and want to try other sports.

It is important to remember, however, that the number one reason athletes with promising talent and bright future in a sport quit is an overemphasis on competition. This virtually always comes from coaches or parents originally. This pressure may be overt and abusive from coaches or parents or it may be more subtle. Subtle pressure can be thought of as the silent athlete motivation and performance killer. It is very important for the parents to observe their children for signs of harmful overemphasis on competition, usually seen in negative feelings and inexplicable changes in desire for practice or competition.

It is sometimes confusing to parents and coaches when the athlete seems to put more pressure on himself than any adults do. I have worked with numerous young athletes with symptoms of anxiety, dread of going to competition and inexplicable problems that arise which interfere with competition. Frequently, parents will bring their children in and say they can't understand why their child is so driven and ruthless with themselves because the parents and coach don't feel that way. The thing is, kids can do it to themselves. They can get it anywhere; other kids, television or even what they think elders feel, believe or want. No matter where the excessive pressure comes from, it can be equally damaging and needs to be addressed if symptoms appear.

Feelings in competition, which include pressure, is a complicated issue and is also dealt with in other areas in this book to the extent possible. If your child continues to report feeling a lot of pressure or manifests some of the other symptoms of too much pressure, it is imperative to deal with it effectively. This may include seeking the services of a sport psychologist but if you do not address it sufficiently you can expect your child to be miserable, under perform, develop seemingly unrelated problems such as injuries or quit.

One of the biggest keys to success is simple. Keep it fun. If the practice and competition is not fun or at least rewarding in some way, then something is wrong. By fun, I don't mean goofing off. Positive feelings can come in many packages including running harder than you ever have trying to win a race or the reward of working hard to get just a little faster. Keeping training and competition positive and in line with their motivation has too many subtle factors to be addressed comprehensively here. But, by developing a significant understanding of the experience your child is having in their sport and making sure there is a good match to their motivation, you can do a lot to insure that they are having a constructive and rewarding sport experience.

Chapter 7

CONFIDENCE

Introduction

Elizabeth and Angela were teammates on a college softball team. They were about the same size and strength. They trained a lot together and became good friends. They were both great in the field, but there was a big difference at the plate. Elizabeth was very athletic and could really rip the ball, but going to the plate was sheer terror for her. As she went to the plate, her heart was racing. She knew this was a great pitcher. Her palms were sweating. She told herself to relax, but she just knew the pitcher was going to make a fool of her. She waited in the box, telling herself to not strike out as the first strike blew by her. Now she was one down and knew she had to hit the next one. The pitcher seeing Elizabeth was already beaten threw another fastball for her and Elizabeth swung with all her might. Strike two. Elizabeth knew she was really in trouble now, she thought about all the people she was letting down, she could not let another one by, she swung at a curve and missed. Just as she feared, she struck out.

It pained Angela to see her friend in such distress. She knew Elizabeth was every bit as good as her, but Elizabeth didn't know it. Now it was her turn. When Angela looked out on the field, she saw opportunity. She did not care who the pitcher was, she was going to ram it down her throat. She let a close ball go by and hit the next one over the back fence.

Elizabeth looked up from her misery to see her friend hit it out of the park. She thought "Why can't I do that?" The answer for Elizabeth is that she was asking the wrong question. The question should have been "How can I do that?" You may see with reference to the Essential Concepts that Elizabeth did everything wrong at the plate. Confidence is learned and developed according to the laws of mental mechanics. Some time later, Elizabeth did learn how her mind worked and how to use focusing skills to execute at her highest skill level and develop supreme confidence. With a change in focus and feelings, she gained use of her substantial abilities and became the major offensive player that her coach always knew she could be.

Of course the names are changed, but this is a true story. Still, it is only one example of many that follow the same course. In this situation, Angela's confidence was one part of her approach to hitting that contributed to her IPS and resulted in being able to access her resources. Until Elizabeth learned how to think differently, her lack of confidence fed her anxiety which detracted from her IPS making it much more difficult to perform up to her physical potential.

Understanding Confidence

The confidence your child experiences or develops in sports will directly relate to the confidence they will have in almost every area of activity for the rest of their life. This is one reason some parents choose to enter their child into sports, so that they can have a controlled environment with direct feedback in which to develop their confidence skills. Confidence is also both general and situation specific. People experience varying levels of confidence in different areas of life. Even if a child enters a sport with no knowledge of that sport, they can hone their skills at achieving mastery and building confidence as they learn. Your child will bring a certain level of confidence to the sport situation, but the quality of the sport environment and the way your child comprehends it can have a significant impact on the confidence they feel and develop.

Some athletic environments are more conducive to developing confidence and other positive personality attributes and some are less so. For this reason, it is important for you to understand the psychological factors at work so you can assess, and impact as needed, the quality of your child's sport experience.

What is confidence? There are many definitions and numerous ideas about what confidence entails, but we may find a simple definition most useful at this point. Confidence can be defined as a feeling that one has the ability to respond to a situation in an effective and sufficient manner. We all experience a general level of confidence and then a specific level of confidence with regard to specific activities and situations. Confidence increases the chance of success because it contributes to the IPS where, on the other hand, doubt, fear and anxiety detract from the IPS.

Athletes want to feel confident or comfortable that they can get it done and lack of confidence is a huge stressor. Athletes find it easier to execute well when they feel confident, but most feel changing their level of confidence is outside their control, other than by the old method of creating a history of successful executions. Most confidence is created by the athlete observing that they had been successful in that situation in the past, which leads to an expectation that they would be successful in that same situation in the future. This method presents problems when lack of confidence makes it hard to obtain success they can use to create confidence. You can see the problem with this approach and why lack of confidence has been such a difficulty for athletes. But understanding mental mechanics offers another way.

We talk about confidence as something we have, which is actually not true. Confidence is not really something we have, it is something we create in our mind and then experience. When you think about it, almost all of that which we experience emotionally is something we are creating in our mind at that moment. One person could look out at a brown field and feel sad that it had died. Another person, who knew the field had just provided a rich harvest leaving only dried up sticks, would feel good as they looked upon it. One person might emerge from a car wreck angry because their new car got wrecked. Another person could emerge joyous that they had walked away from a car wreck intact.

The confidence your child feels will be determined by how they look at the situation and their assessment of their ability to successfully respond. Confidence is something experienced in the moment and that is also where you find the control, in your moment to moment thoughts, to determine how much confidence you will feel.

Developing Confidence

Although I cannot recreate here all the things I do to help athletes gain confidence while working with them on the court or in my office, I hope to give you some ideas you can use with your athlete. The first step with which we have already begun is the understanding that confidence is not something we have, but is something we create from moment to moment. With the awareness that we create confidence or the opposite, performance anxiety, we can move beyond feeling a victim of our feelings to feeling we are in control because we create our feelings. The following discussion of ideas may help you understand the process a little more in order to help you build consistent confidence in your athlete.

Entertain the idea of seeing the situation differently. This process is called cognitive reframing. During the Apollo 13 emergency, it was said to the flight director "This could be one of our greatest disasters" to which he responded "No, I think this could be one of our greatest moments." If a quarterback was inconsistent, rather than worry, it could be thought that today will be one of the good days. Rather than worry, a hitter could think "Because I struck out the last few times, I am now due to get a hit." The options are endless and you can experiment with optimistic ways to say things. The important thing here is that with an optimistic view, you are not trying to predict the future, you are trying to put a positive spin on it for the purpose of creating the most optimal conditions for something good to happen. If something good does not happen, then everyone concerned can gain some solace from the fact that they did everything possible to create a good process to get something good accomplished, and that useful information can be gained from the attempt so a better attempt can be made in the future.

Another way to respond to low confidence is with what is sometimes called, calling the game. In other words, you can decide to set feelings aside in favor of creating the best chance of getting a hit by understanding that you will have a better chance at the plate by not focusing on outcome, and alternately focus completely in the present on executing the mechanics of hitting that creates the best chance for a hit. In possession of the knowledge that worrying about the outcome of getting a hit, or not, and what that would mean, only creates anxiety which interferes with the IPS, don't focus on it. The key here is to choose to focus only in the present on the process of execution and not on the future outcome. Remember, what we focus on at the moment creates the feelings of the moment. For that moment, nothing else exists in our mind to create feelings. So, not focusing on the future outcome of the current at bat cannot create anxiety or any other detrimental feelings. Understand that you can choose what to focus on, then choose to focus on what will create the state which is best for execution, again the IPS.

If it is disrupting your state, give up the emotional need for the desired outcome. Let it go. You may have seen this many times in life. When you give up on trying to make something happen, it seems to happen right then because you are unleashing your ability to create it.

Another strategy is to change what you consider the outcome to be. This is a different use of reframing. No hitter can be sure they will get a hit which can trigger the emotions that they connect with not getting a hit. I suggest changing to an outcome that you will be guaranteed to achieve. That outcome is results. Continuing this line of thinking, you can consider any results the batter will get as good. If the batter gets a hit, it is one more verification that the process of hitting used will create desired results. If they get a strike, they have just made it more clear what does not work. Failures to achieve desired results that might negatively impact confidence can be alternately understood as a necessary part of the process that all athletes have to go through to figure out what works for them. If they strike out again, that can mean that they needed to experience that to gain more information about how to create success.

In a playoff game, it may be harder to accept a strike as good for learning when all the chips are on the line. At this point, a method to feel comfortable at the plate might be a philosophical view of the situation that amounts to "We do not have complete control. There are others on the team. It is not all up to me. All I can do is give it my best shot and that is all there is to it." If a player then feels that they are doing all they can do to create success at that moment at bat, then they may be able to let go of the demand for a hit. If they let go of the pressure and just swing freely, their chances for success are increased.

Another technique to help the player feel confident when they are going to the plate is to have them remember times in the past when they did well in a similar situation. If they can concentrate well enough to remember vividly or relive the good execution of the past, they will automatically also access the state and good feelings of that moment. If they then move directly to execution and focus only in the present on their execution, some of the performance state including good emotions and confidence from the images of the past will tend to remain and facilitate good execution.

Additional Considerations

I have been making a controversial argument for years that confidence may be overrated. Confidence has always been elusive and although we have discussed some methods to increase confidence, or at least reduce the lack of confidence, it is still somewhat of a challenge to modify it. There are additional advanced mental imagery techniques I can employ in my office that build a confidence base, but those techniques are very technical and far beyond the scope of this book.

Athletes like being confident. There is not doubt that feeling confident makes it easier to execute with the higher level of abilities that have been developed up to the time of execution. However, when you think about it, executing correctly is what gets the job done. The mental training concepts reviewed in this book deal directly with the behavioral components that create good execution. If these processes are employed, such that the physiological and attentional goals that comprise the IPS are met, good execution will result. My argument is that if an athlete is completely focused on these processes and not on their lack of confidence, they will forget the thoughts and feelings related to lack of confidence. The forgotten thoughts and feelings about confidence will not interfere with their IPS resulting in a higher chance that they will execute with a high level of their skill and create their best chance of achieving success. By the way, although this is a strategy, I am not saying it is easy.

A personal example may help to make this concept a little easier to use. I was playing a round with a professional golfer who was a prospective client. I have found that in golf amateur golfers tend to expect me to play a good game of golf because I am a sport psychologist. Professionals do not expect as much because they fully understand how difficult it is, but if I choke under pressure, their confidence in me may come into question. We were teeing off on a hole straight out of most golfer's nightmares. It was over a long water hazard to a narrow uphill fairway with lots of bad trouble to the left and right. For the non golfer, this is about as stressful as a tee shot gets. Golfers might be feeling stressed already just thinking about it.

If I thought about the outcome, I could have lost confidence and proceeded into fear and anxiety which would make it much more difficult to execute. But, following sport psychology theory, my solution was to forget about outcome and focus totally in the present with the few swing thoughts I believed would create a good swing. For golfers, the thought was to come down on plane and get through the ball. That was it, no outcome thoughts at all. I did exactly that and was successful with a great shot which drew compliments from the pro. The point here is that I did not have to even deal with confidence. I called the game on confidence and focused in the way that I knew would give me the best chance of success. During the execution, I was focused 100% in the present on execution. In retrospect, I don't think I was feeling anything. As was previously discussed, remembering this successful execution can actually be used to build confidence, but at the time of execution, confidence was not a factor. An argument can be made that I had confidence that my focus would give me the best chance of a good shot. This may be true but it could also be said that I was depending on my belief or expectation that it would be the most productive method to create results and there was nothing more that I could do. Another way to describe the ease in producing good results would be that I was able to focus on a couple of specific tangible actions devoid of emotion that were relatively under my control. This is getting a little theoretical but my hope is that it may provide alternative seeds of thought that may be useful to you.

Although athletes prefer to feel confident and confidence can assist in execution, it is also possible to understand confidence as a side effect of execution. When you think about how confidence is traditionally built, that makes some sense. Traditionally in basketball when a player had a lot of confidence, it was because they had a history of shooting well. When a player went into a shooting slump, it would usually start with some misses. The player would lose confidence and things would begin to slide downhill. The coaches would usually tell them to "keep shooting and it would eventually come back." This is called a shooters mentality. The player would then keep shooting and eventually they would hit a few, become more confident, they would continue to hit more frequently and then eventually get back on track. Sometimes the coach might remind them they had shot well which might give them a little confidence boost and move them toward their IPS. Their full confidence would return when they were hitting their average again, as a side effect.

The point is, that it may be useful to think about confidence in different ways. Although having confidence facilitates execution, it is also a side effect of execution. De-emphasizing it as an important precondition of success may have significant value. This is particularly true and potentially a valuable tool in the case of an athlete who cannot experience confidence for one reason or another.

In my many years of practice, I have found that when I first focus on helping the athlete understand and then enter into their IPS, their performance has increased almost 100% of the time. Although athletes may present with lack of confidence as the main issue, once the situation is reviewed, confidence is rarely the primary focus. Once performance increases, an increase in confidence follows, kind of like the tail on a dog. Feelings like confidence are usually the hardest behaviors of an athlete to change. For most athletes, focusing on physical actions that create success is easier for them to do. Having your athlete let go of attention to confidence and focus only on creation of execution actions might be an effective way to help them deal with the situation of low confidence. As I mentioned before, many of these concepts in mental training are interrelated. You may recall that I stated that I have never found an athlete developing performance anxiety, or having confidence issues, without incorrectly focusing in the past on results they obtained, or in the future on results they might or might not get.

Chapter 8

COMPETITION AND
PERFORMANCE ANXIETY

Introduction

Competition anxiety and performance anxiety are two terms for the same experience prior to performance and are used interchangeably, generally and in this text. The only difference is performance anxiety can apply when there is no direct competition, so is slightly more generic, but both result from concerns the athlete has about the quality or result of their execution in an upcoming event. This anxiety is one of the biggest reasons most individual athletes seek out a sport psychologist. Some athletes experience a light case of "butterflies" which can be ok and may even sharpen their performance. Others experience moderate to severe competition anxiety which is disturbing to the athlete and interferes with their ability to perform, in other words takes them out of their IPS. Teams, on the other hand, mostly request the services of a sport psychologist to maximize their performance, whether to start well, perform at higher levels, maintain consistency under pressure or change a losing trend to a winning one, but performance anxiety is still usually experienced by a number or the players and is dealt with as part of attaining the IPS.

Most athletes and parents seek help too late. This happens for several reasons, from believing that a struggle with anxiety is a sign of weakness to a lack of awareness that competition anxiety can be virtually eliminated. Some still harbor the antiquated belief that seeking assistance from a sport psychologist means the athlete is mentally ill or deficient in some way, which is simply not true. Treating mental illness is totally different than teaching athletes how to be more effective, and many athletes experience performance anxiety. Frequently parents and athletes think it will just go away, but performance anxiety is there because it is created for some reason in the mental processes of the athlete, and until the reason is handled, it usually does not go away and continues to stay around causing difficulties. Frequently, performance gets worse and can create a host of undesirable and unnecessary side effects which may even include the athlete leaving the sport, directly or indirectly, because they are miserable. Unfortunately, I usually see athletes after significant losses in time and other resources have occurred. In reality, performance anxiety is a sign of good motivation that the athlete wants to achieve, but the sign has terrible effects on the athlete. Many of the tools and methods an athlete can use to redirect the anxiety into productive thoughts and behaviors are contained in the mental training program discussed in this book.

Understanding Performance Anxiety

We have all witnessed competition anxiety. It will be helpful to agree on a common definition for competition anxiety as "anxiety that an athlete feels in anticipation of a competition, just before competition or during parts of the competition." Notice that you never hear about athletes experiencing anxiety after competition because anxiety is all about concern about what will happen in the future.

Just like confidence, it is important to understand that anxiety is not something we have like a soccer ball. It is an experience that we create in the moment in response to fear that we will not get some outcome that we desire. Herein lies our opportunity because the fact that anxiety is created by what we do, essentially our thinking, leads to the inevitable conclusion that if we stop doing the things that create anxiety, we won't have anxiety. Anxiety is created by what we think, believe, expect and mostly fear.

Anxiety has a mental and physiological component; but it is created exclusively through undesirable mental function. This and other chapters discuss how the thoughts, beliefs and resulting feelings create anxiety. Alternative mental activity creates the opposite of anxiety. This is the Ideal Performance State which is a fearless and optimal way to approach competition.

Competition anxiety includes worry and fears about not performing up to some criteria in an upcoming competition and can include physiological disturbances such as upset stomach, shaking, sweaty palms, sleep disturbance and irritable or unstable moods. It is not uncommon for athletes with pre-competition anxiety to experience headaches, physical problems or otherwise become ill without their conscious intention. Some have tried to deal with it by reducing expectations or avoiding competition. This is not a good solution and secondary problems with long term consequences can result.

Many of the same symptoms of anxiety can be found both in pre competition anxiety and anxiety during the competition, but there are usually some differences. Prior to the competition, anxiety can be disruptive to the comfort and health of the athlete, while setting them up for poor performance. During the competition anxiety will frequently actually interfere with performance. Anxiety can interfere with mental functions such as concentration and decision making that we see manifesting in ways such as mental errors, committing fouls and missing reads and keys. Because it changes the physical status of the athlete, anxiety can interfere with the IPS by inducing tightness which can change muscle movements and alter form in execution resulting in an ineffective execution. Examples of these problems can be missed shots in basketball, bad throws or catches in football, ineffective swings or bad pitches in baseball, subtle alterations in form or timing leading to bad golf swings, reduced reaction time and slow punches in boxing. It can be some comfort to those that have trouble sleeping due to pre-competition anxiety that one study found that loss of sleep the night before competition did not adversely affect the performance of elite runners, but a good sleep is always better. Once the competition anxiety issue has been dealt with sufficiently, the athlete will be able to sleep well and it is always better to start with a good night's sleep.

Fear is the cognitive/emotional part of anxiety and includes fear of failure, fear of performing poorly and fear of what these failures will to mean to the athlete and others. These fears give rise to the physical parts of anxiety. Fear and the physical symptoms of anxiety are a natural human reaction to thoughts of worry about something bad happening to us. They are components of the natural fight or flight response that is hard wired into humans. Over human history, the fight or flight response has served humans well by preparing them to fight more effectively or run when needed. Fear and anxiety about being killed during a hunt of dangerous game caused ancient man to prepare with sharpened spears and create tactics to increase the chance of safety and success.

Fear is included in the list of possible clues that an athlete may be experiencing performance anxiety due to its prominent role in performance anxiety. Not only is fear a symptom that we can observe; but fear of some type of outcome not being what the athlete wants it to be is at the root of most, if not all, competition anxiety.

Symptoms of Performance Anxiety

Symptoms of performance anxiety you might see in your child vary greatly and include, but are not limited to, the following:

Expressions of worry about performance and fear of failure
Concern about not appearing to be a good player
Concern about others observing that the athlete is nervous
Fear of being seen as a failure, inadequate, incompetent or weak
Fear of embarrassment
Poor decision making on the field and missing important information such as reads and keys

Sometimes, problems that appear to be unrelated physical experiences may be caused by stress and performance anxiety and include:

Trouble sleeping
Irritability and problematic interactions with family and friends

Shortness of breath
Rapid breathing or hyperventilation
Dizziness or confusion
Problems concentrating or focusing on the task
Heart palpations or rapid heart beat
Excessive sweating
Fatigue
Poor physical endurance
Nausea before and during early parts of the game

Assessing Performance Anxiety

Care must be taken in concluding that competition anxiety is present. Some of the behaviors described in the above list can be caused by other things so sufficient understanding of the athlete's experience should be gained before decisions on a remedy are made. A great number of the symptoms noted above can indicate medical problems so it is important to investigate that avenue thoroughly before you investigate psychological causes

If you have concerns about anxiety the first thing to do is talk to your athlete. I suggest picking a not stressful time to have a relaxed conversation with your athlete about the thoughts and feelings they have during training and especially before and during competition. Although I have said it other places, it is so important I must mention it here, wait until the intensity and emotions have calmed down after training or competition to talk to the athlete about this. Examine their experiences in light of the concepts discussed in this book and be supportive of the things that seem healthy while looking into the things that cause you concern. A good strategy is to notice any differences between the state they describe in different situations, explore the impact of the changes and investigate the source of any changes that concern you. The chapter on communicating with your athlete gives you guidelines that will make this data gathering conversation much more comfortable and productive for you and your athlete.

If you still are not sure what is going on but undesirable mental or physical symptoms seem to be present, this may be a good time to consult a clinical sport psychologist that you can trust. Evaluating if a professional is a good choice for you is discussed further in the chapter about choosing a sport psychologist but I just want to say here please make an informed decision before you enlist the services of a sport psychologist or someone trying to fill this role. I suggest getting recommendations and interviewing the sport psychologist before you decide to work with them. I always offer to speak with the parents on the telephone or in person at no charge before I meet with an athlete or family to answer their questions, to make sure I am the best professional to serve them and to help them feel comfortable with the process. Frequently parents or athletes will be concerned that seeing a sport psychologist means they have something wrong with their mind. But, once they understand the nature of the situation all these concerns disappear and they become excited that they are learning solutions to disturbing situations and mental skills that can make them more effective for the rest of their life.

Eliminating Performance Anxiety

Fortunately, many symptoms of competition anxiety can be reduced or eliminated relatively easily by understanding their nature and with application of mental training procedures. The

Essential Concepts identify types of thinking that will get the athlete in trouble by creating anxiety and offers alternative ways to think that lead instead to the IPS. Recall that it was suggested that the best athlete focus is always in the present except for some isolated tasks such as scouting, planning and coaching. During a competition, a movement of focus from the present to the past or future outcomes damages performance by distracting the athlete from focusing on execution and may disturb the IPS. All desirable results come from focusing in the present on what you are doing while you are doing it.

Fear of failure is discussed in another chapter but incorrect use of self-talk, beliefs and expectations can all create anxiety. Shakespeare stated that "expectations are the root of all heartache." There are many variations of thought that can create anxiety. The point here is to identify what thinking creates anxiety and then find alternative mental activity that does not lead to anxiety. The important message here is that anxiety is a result of mental activity. By identifying the thoughts that create anxiety and changing them, you can mostly eliminate performance anxiety. Fear and anxiety are responses created by focusing out of the present and into the future with a concern that things may not go as desired. Other than some planning, nothing gets done out of the present. If an athlete is having fear fantasies or anxiety regarding the future, coach them not to think about the future and focus in the present on what they can do to create what they want. As was mentioned in Essential Concepts, thoughts of the future should mostly be avoided with the exception of a general thought, belief and expectation that things will go well. This reduces the development of anxiety and facilitates development of the IPS; thereby increasing the chance that they will do well.

If for some reason, anxiety has not been eliminated, the physical symptoms of anxiety can be reduced by use of mental focusing skills directed at reducing the physiological arousal of anxiety and simultaneously inducing the relaxation response. A person cannot feel anxiety and relaxation at the same time. When control is exercised to create relaxation, physiological symptoms of anxiety disappear. Frequently, because the mind and body are connected, so do mental experiences of anxiety. A good example is a star player on a soccer team that I was working with on an ongoing basis. Several games into the season, I discovered that he had vomited before every game. I had been teaching his team how to use mental skills to sharpen execution for some time and I only needed to tell him how he could use the physical mental focusing skills to relax before the game. He was able to apply the skills without further instruction and never felt sick again. What he was thinking that created the extreme physiological arousal could have been investigated, but in this context being able to adjust his energy level to the ideal level was sufficient. His performance actually increased, possibly because he was able to keep needed food energy in his stomach or maybe because he was just more comfortable or felt more in control.

In summary, as performance anxiety is created by the athlete in their mind, performance anxiety can be eliminated in the same place by changing mental activity. By applying the basic principles of mental mechanics discussed in the Essential Concepts sections, alternative ways to think can be found that are logical, justifiable and that will create the IPS as an alternative to the state of performance anxiety. Although it may take some time and work to understand and change mental processes, it is very worthwhile. Doing so not only virtually eliminates performance anxiety but also results in an automatic and frequently significant increase in performance. Of course, the information in this book cannot address the myriad of situations that you may encounter; but it is hoped that it will give you a basis from which to develop some useful responses to performance anxiety. Aspects of this topic are also addressed in other chapters and you may find additional information there that may assist you in discovering valuable solutions.

Chapter 9

DEALING WITH PRESSURE

Understanding Pressure

We have all felt pressure before, the feeling that we really need to win and if we don't, it will be awful. Maybe it was struggling with the fear of getting tense on the first tee and hitting a bad shot. Maybe it was when preparing to shoot a free throw with the game on the line. The level of pressure an athlete can experience can run from very light, which can sometimes actually help, to a level that is debilitating.

Although feeling pressure is often experienced along with performance anxiety and fear of failure, looking at it in isolation here may help you understand more clearly how it is developed and how to stop or avoid it

I have worked with many child athletes experiencing pressure and all the negative effects that follow when pressure is not handled properly. Frequently the mystified parents have told me that they did not put pressure on their children, but they seem to feel it anyway. Parents are surprised to learn that this is not an uncommon situation due to the fact that kids are very good at creating pressure, even without any help from parents and coaches.

Pressure can come from many sources. Sometimes, coaches and parents do put pressure on the athletes to perform in very direct ways. This is one of the easiest forms of pressure to observe and decrease, if the source of the pressure is open to receive feedback that their behavior is leading the athlete to feel pressure. Very frequently though, the pressure from others including parents, coaches, teammates or other sources in the environment is unspoken, making it less easy to recognize and harder to cope with effectively. Many parents do not realize how deeply their 12 year olds think about the impact of their participation in sport on the family and feel pressure from it. This is something parents need to watch for. Without the parents ever saying the sport is costing a lot or speaking about having to make sacrifices, the children often think about it anyway. They are very good at picking up this type of concern and if they are thinking about it, they may take actions on these perceptions that are in the best interest of no one.

One figure skater in an elite program stated that she was losing interest in her sport and wanted to scale back her training. In truth, it was found that she was feeling both pressure to perform and guilt for using up so much family resources such that she had actually convinced herself that she was losing interest in the sport. After her concerns were recognized and the situation discussed with her while providing assurances that everyone else was ok, her excitement and passion for the sport returned. This is more frequently encountered toward the elite levels where the financial and time expenditures are much higher, but can be found at any level. Even at high school sports levels, kids can have concerns about the time and money spent by their parents on their sport impacting the family and resources available to other siblings.

Kids naturally want to perform well to please their parents and coaches. This is good and desirable at a certain level, but problems develop when this desire becomes so prevalent and so strong that it becomes a distraction and fuels the development of fear of failure and competition anxiety. Feeling pressure, fear of failure and competition anxiety can cause a variance from the IPS and result in effects ranging from not performing up to the level of their ability to serious emotional and physical difficulties.

Sources of Pressure

The key to understanding pressure and also dealing with it is recognizing the fact that pressure is all in our own mind. Although external sources of pressure such as coaches, parents or the media may tell the athlete in many ways how much they need to perform well, it is the thinking of the athlete that creates the feeling of pressure. It is when the athlete thinks that they must achieve a certain level of play or something bad will happen that the feelings of pressure in the form of performance anxiety or other unpleasant effects can develop. Like many of the things we are discussing, if it is created in the mind, it can be uncreated in the mind or avoided. Remember, just because someone does something, it doesn't mean they have to continue doing it when a better way is found.

There are many thoughts and beliefs that create the feeling of pressure to perform, but a partial list includes:

I have to do it.

I have done it before so I must do it every time or I am no good.

I have to win for: parents, coaches, school, teammates, friends and any other outside entities.

I have to win or I am no good, a failure or a disappointment.

I must win or something bad will happen, from people feeling bad to a loss of something.

If I do not perform to some criteria, then all the money, effort or resources are wasted.

Reducing Pressure

Essentially, any thought that results in a belief that a certain outcome must be reached or something bad will happen is a recipe for pressure. The antidote for performance pressure is to counter the belief that a certain thing must happen with an alternative belief that it does not have to happen. Reality really helps here because it is rarely true that the athlete absolutely has to have the specified outcome or all will be lost as they believe, so you can usually come up with a good argument. A key factor is changing what they see as a need that they must get met, to a want. Yes, it is true that it would be good to show up well for the scout or good to win the playoff game, but an argument can almost always be made that things will be ok if it does not happen. There is far less pressure when pursuing something a person wants as opposed to something they must have to avoid some unacceptable outcome.

If your athlete tells you in one way or another that they are feeling pressure, you can usually follow the three step process that moves athletes from a debilitating fear and anxiety state that has been created to the productive focus that will create their best chance of success, the IPS. If your athlete tells you that they "just have" to have a certain outcome you can start the process by just saying "no, you don't." They may think you are crazy, but you will definitely have their attention which is the first step in helping them see the world from a different perspective. The second step is to get them to change their "have" to a "want." You can then proceed to make the argument that the world will not end, they won't die of disappointment and other things they worry about can be seen in a different way such that things will still be good if they don't get what they think they need to have. A 17 year old rookie in a recent golf match was swinging freely, playing like she did not have a care in the world, that is, without pressure. Not surprisingly, she was performing extremely well in a situation where other established professionals were struggling with the pressure of the big match. Her response to how she could be so relaxed was "I decided a long time ago that I won't die if I hit a bad shot." As they say, out of the mouth of babes, but it can be as simple as that, if that is what a person truly believes.

If the athlete feels they must be successful to make others happy or avoid disappointment, you may be able to turn the need they feel to achieve certain results into a want by a discussion of responsibility for feelings. Most people do not understand very clearly that they are not responsible for another individual's feelings and other people are not responsible for theirs. Understanding that they create the feeling in their own mind and body, that their experiences are responses to what they see, hear and messages they receive from others often serves to help relieve the athlete of the burden they feel. What we feel is, to a great extent, created by our perspective. For example, one student who had been struggling might be happy to get a B on a test; where another student may be unhappy that it was not an A, depending on their perspective.

Coaching an athlete to not feel responsible for the feelings of others followed by turning the focus to the things they can do to create what they "want" to happen can be a major key in taking the pressure off. If the pressure is relieved momentarily by the first step, the second step in this formula takes them farther from their fear and to a focus on an action plan. Focusing on what they have control over and what they can actively do to get the results they want creates an action oriented plan which takes them away from focus on passive worry and gives them the best chance to achieve their intended result.

Sometimes, athletes will feel pressure because they believe their level of success in competition determines their value or defines them as a person. After you tell them it does not, you can help them identify a better basis for feeling good about themselves which is not dependent on an uncertain outcome. You can follow this by helping the child feel that they are loved, appreciated, and respected equally no matter what the outcome. Due to the impact of a society that goes in the opposite direction, this may need to be communicated multiple times. This does not mean that we do not desire our child to do a clean program, hit a great dive, or win a race. It feels great to achieve and win, but by creating an atmosphere where the athlete feels there is no "down side" or that they do not have a great deal to lose, they become emotionally free to focus on being their best.

The traditional response to pressure was to treat it as something that we could be tough about or just push through and then things would be much easier. Fortunately, with greater understanding of pressure, we can now create a more elegant and effective response that can virtually eliminate it. Assessment of pressure is easily accomplished by talking with the child about their feelings so you can see if they express competition worries or other symptoms of stress or pressure. Although we reviewed several methods that athletes create pressure and discussed ways to alleviate the pressure, there are many more common pathways to experiencing pressure we did not discuss. However, the basic mechanism by which athletes create pressure is the same. By talking with your child about their experience, you may be able to discover the way they implement the pressure pattern and help them shift to another perspective where pressure is minimized or eliminated.

Chapter 10
FEAR OF FAILURE

Introduction

Aside from catastrophic injury, fear of failure is one of the most damaging things an athlete can experience in sports. Fear of failure has been said to "handcuff" an athlete and can be at the root of a huge number of undesirable, and at times seemingly unrelated, feelings and behaviors. It is frequently the reason athletes lose big competitions and competitions where they had a very good chance of winning. Fear of failure is a major component of competition anxiety which we know can rob the athlete of enjoyment in their sport and decrease their ability to train and compete most effectively. For this reason, it is critical for you to be certain that your child understands the concepts of success and failure in the most useful way. I acknowledge that it can be very difficult to deal with, but it is worth the effort to address it and eliminate it as much as possible.

Fear of failure can lead to competition anxiety, not giving full commitment and effort, self imposed limitations, undesirable choice of goals and a host of other undesirable choices by the athlete; thereby derailing their ability to reach their potential and get the most from their investment in irreplaceable time, money and energy. Whether the goal is to enjoy participating or achieve specific numbers or placement, fear of failure is an avoidable pitfall. A constructive understanding of this concept can significantly facilitate productive training and the ability to compete at the highest levels of ability where an unconstructive understanding can terribly reduce the quality of training and make competition a stressful, disappointing, discouraging and less productive experience.

Recall the example of the softball players Angela and Elizabeth. If Elizabeth had not learned how to think differently and get beyond the fear of failure, she would never have experienced the success of which everyone knew she was capable. Raw talent got her on the college team. The fear of failure she created as she considered the tougher competition at this level may have cost her the scholarship and remained in her mind as a failure experience for the rest of her life. When Elizabeth was helped to understand what was going on in her mind, and how to think and operate differently, she became able to use here resources and achieve her potential. This was an important turning point in her life. As I said, this is essentially a true story, but it is not the only one. The joy I have seen repeatedly in an athlete and family when blocks to performance and living out one's potential are bypassed, even at the club sport level, is hard to describe adequately.

Do not, by any means, assume your child has it right. Harmful understandings of success and failure are rampant in out society and actually facilitated by it. After the last Olympics, a talk show host said to an American athlete "how does it feel to have lost the gold?" To her credit, she immediately responded with "I didn't lose anything, I won the silver." I was really pleased to see she understood the situation, maybe she helped to educate the much older but less wise talk show host. Sadly, we can find many destructive statements all around us such as the stupid statement that I saw on a tee shirt "second place is the first loser." We must combat ignorance to create a healthy and optimally productive mindset for our children.

It is probably obvious, if the child feels like a failure they will not be happy, which is detrimental in child sports, and it will do nothing but push them away from more desirable behavior. It may not be readily apparent, but if you follow the negative feeling you perceive to the source, you can deal with it. Negative feelings most frequently have something to do with failure. In the past, it was more prevalent for parents and coaches to use negative motivation. This includes things like making disparaging comments to the child in an attempt to make them work harder. In the past it was not uncommon for coaches to tell athletes "you can't do it" or "you aren't man enough to do it." Unfortunately, this has, at times, led the child to work harder which encouraged use of this type of motivation. But this negative reinforcement can easily cause terrible side effects that make it a severe mistake in the big picture. In fact, this kind of negative input is one of the more virulent causes of unhappiness among athletes. It is very easy for negative statements or attitudes to be absorbed by young athletes and contribute to issues about failure and help them feel that they actually are a failure as a person. Statements need to be looked at carefully where a comment sometimes used with males such as "its time to man up" could be helpful by encouraging a "take charge" or be tough mindset for one athlete, but in other athletes have a counter productive effect, depending on how it is perceived by the athlete.

What is Failure

So what is failure? The key to eliminating almost all fear of failure is to think about failure in a different way. Consider the following: in one of the last Olympics, Alexander Karelan, the super heavy weight wrestler from Russia lost the gold medal to American Rulan Gardner. Karelan was a monster at 335 pounds with body fat so low he had a six pack. He had never lost a match up until this time. Gardner won the match one point to zero. Even after the match, Gardner said that if he saw Karelan coming down the street that he would move to the other side. So, who won? Clearly, we can say Gardner did because he got the gold medal.

So if Gardner is a winner, is Karelan a loser? He lost the gold medal so does that make him a failure? If he won the next Olympics, would that take him from being a failure to being a winner? He lost the gold but won the silver. Does that make him a winner or a loser in this Olympics? Is he a success or failure?

A common answer would be confusion or it depends. However, this answer will not help your athlete be successful unless it is further broken down into a productive way to look at failure that they can understand and use.

To investigate this concept, let us begin with the simple and literal definition: "success is the attainment of the intended goal and failure is not reaching the intended goal." It usually follows that a person who attained the goal of winning or first place is considered to be a success while every other person who did not is considered a failure. Implicit in this view is that success is good and the athlete should feel good about himself. Additionally, failure is bad and athletes should feel some type of negative emotion about it. You do not need to teach your athlete this definition. They will inevitably get this narrow and mostly toxic understanding from society. Until you discuss this subject with your athlete you will not know what toxic beliefs about training and competition they have absorbed from their environment. After your have discovered them, helping your athlete to turn a toxic belief into a constructive belief can help free them from the burden of the fear of failure.

Individualized Understanding and Models of Failure and Success

Beliefs, perceptions and conclusions are the filters that color our comprehension of the world around us. It is important to understand that as children grow from infants to adults they figure out what is going on in the world and what means what. This understanding of who people are, what these people mean to them, what their relationship is to them, how to deal with them, definitions of concepts such as failure and how the world works becomes their map of reality that they use to get around and create their life. This understanding of the world or map of reality is also often called the individuals Model of reality. Everyone uses their model or map of reality to understand and interact with the world. But just like a road map is not an exact representation of the territory, there have to be some deletions and there may be mistakes, an individuals map of reality is also subject to deletions, distortions, over and under generalizations and conclusions that may not be completely accurate or optimal. To the extent that an individual has an accurate and constructive map, they will have a good start on being effective. The importance here is that everyone's map is created by them and if inefficiencies are found, they can be changed. These maps of reality exist mainly at the unconscious level, are frequently not within our awareness, are accepted uncritically once formed, but determine what we focus on, what we believe things to mean and how we evaluate events inside and outside our body. In other words, the map of reality we develop at an unconscious level determines what we perceive, what we feel and the choices we make. The singer Bonnie Raitt has a line in a song you may have heard, "we only see the world we make."

Most people in a given society develop maps which are very similar that allows them to communicate with a common language, follow accepted norms in behavior and perceive things in a similar way, which forms a basis for them to operate relatively effectively in their environment. However, everyone has some differences in their maps due to different experiences in their developmental years. For example, a botanist driving along the road might notice the type of trees he passes and have thoughts about their general health where another person may drive past the trees without even noticing them. People from one culture may have trouble just getting along in a culture with far different beliefs and norms than the one they grew up in. The territory is the same for everyone, but their maps of it are different to a greater or lesser extent.

Toxic Beliefs in the Model
The importance here is that toxic beliefs that interfere with the welfare of an athlete exist in their model because they were learned, and therefore, they can be unlearned and replaced with beliefs and understanding that create better results. We have already reviewed some toxic beliefs generally accepted in society but there are a couple more of special interest here.

Toxic belief number 1. Failure is not an option.

Baloney. The intent is right, which is to create total commitment to the act, but the execution of the idea is wrong. Failure to achieve goals is an inevitable outcome of striving for them while challenging ourselves in the process. We will deal with failure even more frequently and in a more intensive way if we are pushing the limits to excel. A slalom ski racer once told me that if he wasn't falling in training then he wasn't pushing hard enough. Interestingly, when he did fall, it was usually a controlled fall which was not a problem. One type of weight lifting exercise which is very productive for rapid development incorporates the concept of doing "sets to fail" which means going to the point where you cannot do any more. In these situations, the athlete accepts that failing to reach a goal is an expected part of the process and they are emotionally fine with it. Or you could say they work to reach the goal, which is to fail to be able to do more reps, and it is good.

Toxic belief number 2. If I do not reach my goal then I am a failure.

There are several problems with this belief. First of all, a person should never define himself by some outcome. Recall the example of Alexander Karelan, depending on how you look at it we could consider him a success or a failure at many levels. The best way out of this is not to believe that what we just did determines or defines who we are. If we played the best game of our life but our team lost, does that make us a loser? No, a better way to look at this is that there are several outcomes, we did great and maybe hit all our performance goals, which as a member of the team is what we wanted to contribute, but another outcome is that our team lost the game.

Toxic belief number 3. If I did not play my best, then I should feel bad about myself for not doing what I know I can do.

Why? The disappointment of not achieving the goal or reward is enough to feel bad about. Why punish yourself? A better focus would be to focus on the execution components and isolate the changes that need to be made to achieve the desired level of execution in the future. As coach Maxwell tells his football team with a win or loss "we did better, but we're not there yet, we are just trying to get better every time."

Reframing

This leads us to another important way we can eliminate fear of failure. A great way to eliminate fear of failure is to never fail. This is, of course, the athlete's dream but we just discussed how athletes consistently do not reach many of the goals they set. The way to never fail is a secret that few know, but once learned, can revolutionize their experience. The secret is to redefine the sport situation, and specifically, what we regard as winning and losing. This is the technique from clinical psychology known as "reframing."

Remember that we are using a definition of success as achieving the desired goal. The goal is usually seen to be winning the contest. We will be successful every time if we redefine our goal from this common and limited idea of success to a goal that we will always attain, which is results. If our goal is to achieve results, we will never need to feel fear of not obtaining it. In a tennis match, one result is winning the match but there are many other results of our efforts to execute. A win comes from a combination of many things including; effort, concentration, execution of shots, effective strategy, conditioning and the like. If all the components are good enough to out play our opponent, then we win the point. Enough wins of points, games and sets creates a win in the match. I frequently tell athletes that winning is a side effect of effective execution. Recall that the mental training program describes the components that create the top level of execution, and beyond maximizing these components, there is no more an athlete can do. If an athlete is operating effectively, they can look at the results of their effort and break down their execution into components that worked and identify the changes they want to make in components that did not contribute optimally to success. With the change of focus from victory over the opponent to being excited about obtaining results because they know that is the pathway to winning, they will always be successful in their quest to win, even if the specific contest was still only a step in the right direction of competing effectively enough to win a specific competition.

It seems clear that failure or success is a matter of definition set by the individual and not carved in stone. Different conceptions of success and failure will be of differing value for athletes depending on their unique situation. Mastering basic skills and simply arriving to participate are great victories for many. For others, it might be completing a clean program, for others swimming the hardest race in their life, and for others it might be defined by Olympic gold. Remember from our discussion on motivation, athletes differ regarding what they want to get from sports and what motivates them.

Clearly, fear of failure is created in concert with what we interpret failure to be in our model of the world which leads to what we focus on and value. We have the control within us to learn how to interpret failure differently such that we become not vulnerable to fear of failure. It is for us to choose the understanding that enables or defeats us. In the case of our children, it commonly falls upon the parents to choose for the children or at least guide them to understand the concept of failure in a way that enables them. Although it may be a challenge for them to understand this new way of looking at the situation, such that success and failure are reinterpreted only as results, over the years athletes who did get it have consistently used it to achieve higher levels of success and have a more positive emotional experience. As they say, "life is what we make it."

As in many things, timing is important here. For example, when working with a super heavyweight Olympic wrestler, I found it important to let him walk off and express his anger by himself. After he finished venting his anger, it was much easier to talk about all aspects of the match and much safer. So remember it is important to talk with your child about their feelings regarding a loss when they are not still experiencing the emotional storm of competition. They may even want, or need, to hear your thoughts and feelings after they have had time to calm down. Do not be surprised if they feel like they disappointed you even if you did not feel disappointed. Children tend to do this on their own and it is important for you to tell them how proud you are of them for all the things they did do such as trying hard, being willing to compete, facing a challenge, etc. Don't try to get it all done at once. Once you understand failure for what it is, and repeatedly revisit these concepts in concrete ways that help them cope with loss and feel good feelings, it will eventually sink in and result in them developing a perspective that will be optimally healthy and productive.

Chapter 11

USING VIDEO AND OTHER FEEDBACK

Using feedback

An athlete's level of success, to a great extent, will be determined by the amount of useful feedback about their performance they can obtain combined with their ability to use it effectively. In fact, availability of good feedback puts a limit on the rate of improvement, as well as the level of expertise that an athlete can ultimately reach. I encourage athletes to gather as much relevant feedback as possible up to the ideal level and pay attention to the process of using it effectively. This chapter addresses the significant challenge of obtaining and using good feedback. This is a challenge because rarely do athletes obtain and use feedback at the optimal level, making it impossible for them to train and perform at the level of which they are capable.

Feedback is a generic term defined here as "information that comes to the athlete concerning any part of their execution". Execution can include results, components or quality of technique or any thing they think or do involved in how they played the game. Feedback can be in many forms, from a "good job" said by a coach to the coach identifying what the athlete did right, did wrong and giving them coaching on what they could do better. Feedback can also come from many other sources including parents, friends, times, percentages, ratings and even the media. Any information that gets back to the athlete about their participation in the sport can be considered feedback.

Guidelines for Handling Feedback

There are some guidelines for handling feedback that you may find helpful:

1. Generally, it is desirable to have as much relevant feedback available as possible. However, an athlete can only use a limited amount of feedback at a time so it is important to determine when to access the information, prioritize it and decide how much to deal with at any given time. Too much feedback can create information overload and distract or overwhelm the athlete so it is important to find the right amount to create optimal conditions for improvement.

2. Not all feedback is helpful information. Some may be irrelevant, some may be wrong and some may be harmful or even mean spirited. It is important to work with your athlete to make these judgments and help them feel comfortable rejecting unconstructive feedback.

3. It is not uncommon for a young athlete to expresses reluctance about obtaining feedback. Similar to unmet goals, athletes sometimes become angry or experience other negative feelings about the mistakes they made or

that they did not do better. These unpleasant feelings are based in a belief that they should have done something better. It is important to contradict this erroneous belief because every athlete in history has made mistakes and mistakes are a natural part of trying to get better. It is easy to feel pleased when something works, but it is also possible to feel good about finding things that did not work. Every mistake discovered moves you one step closer to your goal and shows you something you need to know to get there. It has been said that there are a certain number of mistakes that must be made to get to the high level of execution desired; so the sooner the mistakes are made, the sooner the goal will be obtained. These ideas fit with the discussion we had earlier where it was suggested that wins and losses should be considered the same, simply as results that indicate which components of execution to continue and which components need to be changed.

4. Readiness for feedback is a very important issue. Do not shove feedback down an athlete's throat. Ask them if they are ready to review their execution or receive other feedback and respond appropriately to any negative feelings that may be present before you begin. Before providing feedback to your athlete, remember to appropriately consider the timing, attitude and amount. Athletes vary in the type of feedback that is easiest for them to use. Some need to discuss it until they understand it and others can get all they need from viewing video. The important thing is for you to understand the thoughts and feelings of your athlete about feedback and adjust the presentation so that they can use it most effectively.

5. You may need to remind your athlete repeatedly to never feel bad about having done their best effort. If a mistake is seen and the athlete feels bad about it, they may feel sad that they made a costly error. You may need to acknowledge that the error cost something, but then you need to help your athlete understand that this is just how life works and that making mistakes is just a natural and necessary part of the process of improving. When you think about it, isn't it true that if we made a mistake, we really needed to make that mistake in order to learn what is necessary to enable us to do something different? A mistake is made for a reason which needs to be understood so another path can be chosen. You might need to remind your athlete of the essential concept that perfection gives us a direction to go, but not necessarily a goal that can be reached.

6. Generally, feedback should be as specific as possible. An athlete will feel good if you tell them they had a good game but, apart from generally encouraging them, that is not information they can use to improve. On the other hand, if you identify the percentage or number of times they executed specific actions that they were trying to increase or decrease, then that gives them information they can act on. Whenever possible, you want feedback to be "behavioral feedback" which means something you can see and count. Nonspecific feedback might be that they hit well, where specific feedback might be that they stayed patient at the plate and waited for a good pitch to swing on. Other more specific behavioral feedback could include the number of times they executed with the new

technique opposed to the number of times they executed with the old technique they were trying to discontinue. If the athlete did the specific or target behavior 50% in the last game, you could respond positively and congratulate them for that and set a goal of 60% for the next game. For more information on using goals, refer to the section on short and long term goals. There is a value in feedback about things that cannot be counted such as a good attitude or never giving up. This feedback, although difficult to quantify, can sometimes be some of the most important but may take a little more time to discuss in terms of what was observed.

Using Video Feedback

Video feedback is well known as one of the richest sources of information available to the athlete. If it is used correctly, it can provide some of the most valuable information an athlete can get but if it is used incorrectly, it can be a source of shame and bad feelings the athlete will wish to avoid. Research in communication has shown that only a part of the communication between individuals is verbal content. It is said that a larger amount of the message is communicated not with words but nonverbally by activity including tone of voice, rate of speech and body language. Much of this subtle type of information is available to the athlete when they watch themselves.

We have also found that, in cases where athletes do not understand feedback or may not even believe what is being said to them, watching themselves on video can dramatically increase their understanding and acceptance of the feedback. When individuals are playing, there is only a limited amount of time and awareness that can be devoted to observing and remembering what happened. It is frequently amazing how much more athletes can see and understand important things about their behavior in the game when they watch themselves on video.

The only real danger or downside to video can manifest if it is used improperly by the coach, athlete or parent. If an athlete expresses unhappiness about seeing themselves on video, that is a warning flag for you. It is important to deal with this immediately. This is not an indication to stop using it, but rather a signal that there is some error in the way it is being presented, played, reviewed or utilized. It could indicate some type of a lack of acceptance of themselves or their level of performance, or it could be something else. But, whatever it is, it will slow the development of your athlete if it isn't addressed and changed. The way to change it is simply to ask your athlete how they feel about it and then just talk about their feelings about what they see. Eventually, the process by which they are viewing the images that makes it feel negative will become clear. At that time, you can test your creativity at helping your athlete identify other ways to experience viewing the images or information.

It is very important for you, the coach and your athlete not to be critical in a negative way of the performance. This type of attitude will stop or slow development. This is different from the desirable behavior of pointing out mistakes. There is a subtle but enormously important distinction here. Criticism usually includes a belief that the athlete should not have done that, should have done something different, or that it was bad, incompetent or some other pejorative way of regarding the thing they did. Changing the words good and bad to desirable and undesirable is a step in the right direction, but that's not all there is to it. Generally, every athlete will do the best they can every time. Maybe they did better last time and maybe they will do better next time and maybe it is in their ability range to do better. The important thing to understand is that given what was going on in their environment and in their mind, they did the best they could do at the moment. For example, it may be determined that they under performed because they were not concentrating. It does no good to criticize or make them feel diminished for not concentrating. They might just shut down or feel guilty. What can help is to find what they did that caused them to lose concentration and create a plan for what they can do the next time to maintain concentration.

When working with feedback of any kind, be ready to address the most common error made by athletes. The error here is in perception. This is when mistakes discovered while reviewing the performance are seen as bad or when seeing the video feels bad. It is very important for an athlete not to feel bad about making mistakes or be upset with himself for making mistakes that they needed to make to improve.

We would all like to do everything perfectly the first time. The reality is that this is not how it works. We try to do it right but make some mistakes, while other actions are correct. As we previously discussed, all kinds of mistakes are inevitable and, in fact, are a necessary and indispensable part of developing athletic skills and mastery of the sport. It would then logically follow that the sooner we make all the mistakes necessary to reach the level of mastery we wish, the better. Logically this is true, but the process of development is slowed when emotionally the athlete feels bad about mistakes, obsesses over them or has difficulty really understanding the connection between improvement and mistakes. It is the motivation, enthusiasm and directed activity to get it right rather than avoiding the bad feelings associated with making a mistake that should be constantly emphasized.

The more we work on it, the higher percentage of actions we get right. A major goal is to get the athlete excited about seeing what they are doing and finding how they can continue to do the right things or make changes, as opposed to constantly focusing on avoiding the "wrong things." The best way not to do the undesired things is to do the alternate right things first. It may be useful to focus on mistakes to find where the athlete departs from the process that creates desirable actions. This needs to be closely followed with a focus on procedures that create the desired actions. A related discussion that may be helpful in clarifying these concepts can be found in the section on dealing with failure.

In addition to the factors involved in using feedback effectively that were discussed above, the following list of guidelines for reviewing and using video might help you maximize the use of video as a productive tool.

Guidelines for Using Video Feedback

A. Never play the game of "gotcha" with video where the video is used to prove a point leaving the athlete anticipating data that will prove them wrong or you right. The result is that the athlete feels embarrassed, inadequate or guilty about what is seen. A more appropriate attitude is to take an exploratory attitude that every thing found is valuable as something to keep and reinforce or as something that is good to find so it can be deleted as soon as possible

B. Be aware of how your child feels about reviewing video and if negative emotions are found, find a way to turn them to positive. If they have negative feelings, look for the source, probably in the way they are perceiving the information, and find a way, probably based in the Essential Concepts, for them to see the information in a positive light.

C. Look for ways to make the experience fun. You may want to create a general attitude of mutual exploration and a search for nuggets of gold that can tell the athlete what to keep doing and what to change. Many kids will automatically notice the problems and miss the good things. This is an opportunity for you to enhance their self esteem, confidence and motivation by acknowledging the desirable things they do. Remember, much of the strongest and least conflicted motivation comes from desire to accomplish rather than fear of mistakes. It is very important to help them see mistakes as nuggets of gold they can use to find ways to make their performance stronger.

D. It may be valuable for your child to narrate what is going on regarding what they are feeling and thinking. It is not necessary, or even desirable, for you to have a response to each thing they say. The importance is their increased awareness. At times, there may be no need for discussion because just viewing the execution contains what the athlete needs.

E. Be careful your athlete does not get overwhelmed by the amount of information available to them from video. There is so much information that athletes frequently need to review parts of the execution multiple times to find the valuable information. It may be useful to review the video different times for different reasons and it may take a surprisingly long time to process all the information that is available.

F. You must be careful that your athlete does not fall into the trap of thinking they should be able to make all the changes they want the next time out. Many of the components of execution are habit and habits can take some time to change. No change happens without trying, but it may take several tries to get it accomplished and more to get it stabilized. Most human behavior is built in "successive approximations" where a second piece of good execution is added to the first once the first is somewhat reliable and so on. The old adage "Rome was not built in a day" may make sense to you but your child might respond more to the idea that a Christmas tree is trimmed one step at a time. If the athlete feels the changes they want are too large, you may be able to translate the wisdom of the Chinese philosopher Lao Tzu "The journey of a thousand miles begins with one step" to them in some way that they can understand.

G. You may need to resist the urge to pull out video of your child's performance every time your friends come over. Parents are rightfully proud of strong efforts of their children. Some kids might be proud to show off their performance, but the video is a teaching tool and some might feel it is private and if so it is important to respect their wishes.

H. As an alternative, sometimes athletes would rather look at still pictures as opposed to video. The reason for this feeling may be obscure, possibly because it takes less time, but it may be of value to try it. I do not suggest it as an alternative as the volume of information is much less.

We have been discussing ways to use video in the most effective manner, but you may find other ways this rich source of information may be useful to help your child progress. Kids tend to have a different experience of time, memory and perspective than adults so you need to oversee that they keep a reasonable perspective. Every athlete will hit a plateau of varying length at one time or another. If a child falls into thinking they are not improving or that they are not "any good", older video can remind them where they came from and new video can show them what they have accomplished.

Research in the field of learning has also shown us that one of the easiest ways for humans to learn complicated actions is by observing someone else do it well. The technical name for this process is "imitation" which has a different meaning than the common usage of the term. When a young athlete watches a more advanced athlete execute technique, an enormous amount of learning at all levels goes on. For this reason, I encourage young athletes to spend significant time watching videos of high level execution. While coaching gymnastics, we found combining watching video of higher level gymnasts doing a specific skill with mental imagery skills from the mental training program helped the kids learn new gymnastic skills much more quickly.

Sources to provide additional guidelines for the use of video are not easily found. Some of the suggestions regarding use of video have come from the work of Norman I. Kagan, Ph.D. and his seminal work on the video reviewing process called Interpersonal Process Recall (IPR).

Reference: Archer, J. Jr. et al. A new methodology for education, treatment and research in human interaction. **Journal of Counseling Psychology**, 1972, 19, 275 – 281. I became trained in the IPR technique while working as a teaching and research assistant to Dr. Kagan in the medical school at Michigan State University. In the medical school it was used to train physicians and counselors to be more effective in the communication and data gathering process. Since that time IPR has been found to be tremendously valuable as a non-threatening technique to facilitate self-awareness, interpersonal communication and problem solving in a wide range of applications.

Chapter 12

COMMUNICATING WITH YOUR ATHLETE

Communicating is more than talking

Communicating effectively with your athlete is of primary importance because without effective communication, you have at best lost opportunity for the things that could be accomplished and may be on the road to conflict or chaos. This is the reason that many successful corporations and other institutions have workshops on effective communication and conflict resolution. You may feel you have a great relationship with your athlete and good communication and you are probably right. Just because you have a great relationship, that does not mean your communication will always be at the effectiveness level that is most desirable. Youth sports today is full of details and challenges at all levels for parents and kids, so any improvements you can make in the communication process are likely to be rewarded with a better sport experience for you and your athlete. Most of the parents and athletes I see actually do have a good relationship, but I cannot think of one instance where the parents did not have important unanswered questions and there were not some aspects of the communication process that could be improved.

In your role of parent and support system for your child athlete, there are several key areas where effective communication is
so very important. The most obvious of these is the exchange of
information. Usually, there is information you need to get from
your athlete and information they need from you that is critical
for effective operation. Many things can interfere with efficient
exchange of information. When it does not operate well, there
is usually a cost. Effective communication processes using the
skills discussed in this chapter can help significantly when trying
to understand the needs of your athlete. Frequently in competitive sports, children are faced with situations new to them and
they may find it difficult to fully understand their own needs or
to communicate them. The communications skills can make it
easier for you to help them clarify their needs and emotions and
also explore different ways to handle them. Using effective communication skills makes it much easier for you to perform your
role of supporting your athlete and also will contribute to your
athlete becoming aware of and actually feeling the support you
are providing.

Blocks to communication

One of the biggest blocks to communication and also a cause
of additional problems in the relationship between parents and
children in sports are errors in timing of communication. The
biggest problem usually comes when parents try to communicate feedback or get into an important discussion right after the
competition has ended, maybe on the way home in the car. Sound
familiar? Although this seems a logical time to parents because
events are fresh in everyone's mind and everyone happens to
be together in the car, you may want to resist the temptation.
Sometimes it is a good time, but my experience over many years

has shown that most of the time it is not. A solution is to ask the child if it is a good time to talk about it. Even if they say yes and they think it is, they may not be emotionally ready and not be aware of it, so make your own decision. Athletes differ. When I worked with the Army wrestling team, there were a few athletes that could discuss the competition a few minutes after the competition ended. On the other hand, one of the super heavy-weights, a combat veteran, would leave us immediately after the match and no one attempted to approach or talk to him until he returned and engaged us. A good way to begin discussing things with your athlete any time is simply to ask if this is a good time to talk about it. If you observe behaviors or sense feelings of unhappiness or resistance in response to your question, then it is important to deal with the factors that contribute to the negative emotions before moving into discussion or feedback, if you wish to be productive.

Emotional readiness to discuss the contest needs to be assessed and respected on the part of both the parent and child. Not only might the athlete not be emotionally settled enough to communicate productively right after the match, but you might not be either. Again, the best way to determine readiness is to mention it and see what happens. Try what seems to be the best choice, see how it goes and use this information as feedback in making future choices. If you see your athlete or yourself becoming quickly angry or frustrated, it may be that you chose to communicate too soon or it could be another block. If you find you cannot communicate about performance factors immediately, the best choice is to be generally supportive of their effort and work with details later. If it never seems to be a good time then that is an issue that needs to be addressed and explored.

Another block to communication is over involvement of the parents in their child's sport. This factor is discussed in greater detail in the chapter on the parent role, but it is important to understand that heightened emotions that come from not keeping the experience of the child and parent sufficiently separate can be a block to communication. If the child feels they have to perform for you, then this is an additional burden that will usually create problems. It is natural for kids to want their parents to see them perform well and be proud of them, but when it becomes an extra burden, then it needs to be handled. Usually a statement by the parent indicating a primary appreciation for the work they are putting into the sport and competition is a good way to go.

Another block can develop if the parent becomes involved in coaching their child beyond that which is useful. It is true that parents can be a rich source of feedback but it is important to carefully evaluate the readiness, amount as well as type of feedback that will work the best. Many times the parent has expertise in the sport and possibly was the child's first coach. At times this can be useful, but it must be evaluated regarding usefulness at the specific time under consideration and appropriate action taken. If it is judged to be the right time to back off for the best interest of the child, then this action needs to be taken regardless of the feelings of the parent. It is part of the parent's job to deal with both athlete and parent feelings as needed. There is always risk when parents try to be too involved in coaching. The parent child relationship by nature has many highly developed factors which may add complication to the attempt to coach a child and result in problems.

Communication Skills

The basic communication skills you may have seen and employed in many other places apply here too and if used properly will solve 95% of the situations you will run into. They are Suspending Judgment, Active Listening, Exploratory Questioning followed by Identifying and Labeling the Feelings and Thoughts your child has expressed and then ascertaining if that was what they meant. You can recycle the sequence as often as needed until everything has been stated and both parties are certain that their communications are understood.

Keeping an Open Mind and Suspending Judgment

The value of open mindedness or suspending judgment as a tool for successful communication cannot be overestimated. Most unresolved or unsatisfactory communication results from one or more of the parties mistakenly thinking they understand what the other person is trying to communicate, or from closed minded thought and defensiveness.

By suspending judgment, I mean keeping an open mind about everything until the communication is over on both sides. That is, listening to the facts and expression of feelings of the other person in an unbiased way regardless of what you know or think to be true. In this, as well as other communications, I do mean keeping an open mind to **everything**! Although it is problematic to have a deficiency in information, by far the biggest problem in communication is when people accept as truth and reality, something that is not true. Most people, parents and children, are not as good at this as they think they are, so a dedicated effort is often needed. Usually, you will find that in all but the simplest of matters, if you really listen, their story is somewhat different than what you expected. Even subtle differences can be important. Those who do not resist the temptation to think they know what will be said before the communication is concluded frequently find that the conversation has become misdirected and the child is angry from feeling that they are not being heard or understood.

There is plenty of time after everything has been communicated to state your opinion, so be patient. It may be the same opinion you started with, and you may have heard what you expected to hear, or not. The difference is that if you listen with an open mind, the child will feel that you care enough about them and their message to listen. If you do not agree, they will be more open to hear what you have to say after they feel they have been heard. Many communications are doomed to failure in the first few moments when openness to their communication and a lack of judgment is not experienced by the child. As a reminder, openness is communicated not only by words but also nonverbally by voice quality and body language. If you think you are fooling your child, you're probably not. It is often useful for one parent to observe the other parent and give them feedback on how they appear during communication with their children.

Active Listening

Active listening is the skill of helping the other person communicate their message completely to you without causing them to change their meaning and also letting them know you understood what they meant. Just because you understand what they are saying does not mean they know you understand, so it must be actively communicated. Many times kids have shrugged off communication with their parents saying something like "There is no use talking when nobody is listening, so I just quit trying" or simply feeling that their parents just don't care. This is a guaranteed formula for problems. I have rarely seen a significantly troubled parent/child relationship where the parents had the ability to listen effectively.

The first thing to do after determining the timing is right to communicate is create a comfortable environment. Make sure you listen patiently in a relaxed manner and with an open mind to what they are saying. It may be helpful to break a long discussion into the smallest pieces necessary to assure full understanding of each piece until you have gone through the entire communication.

After you have patiently listened to what your child has to say, the next step is to communicate back to the child what you think they said to check the accuracy of your perception. Depending on the type of material, the best way to do this is to either repeat the details of what they said or paraphrase back to them what you thought they meant. Then ask "is that what you meant?" If they say that you understand what they are communicating, you can continue on to the next part of the communication. If they say something like "no that's not really it", you can ask them to tell you again, maybe in different words. After they communicate again, you can continue with the same process of checking out if you really understood what was meant and continue with this process until they tell you that you have it right.

If your version of what they said is accurate, then they will feel heard and understood. If your version of what they said is inaccurate, they still feel good that you are trying and the conversation is facilitated as they try other ways to explain what they mean. When your version of their communication is correct, it makes them feel good and you have a large amount of accurate information.

Make sure they do not feel it is a failure on their part if you do not understand. Just tell them communication can be complicated and it sometimes just takes a while to make sure everyone completely understands what everyone means. Usually kids feel good that you are taking the trouble to fully understand what they mean. Often, they might not fully understand what they are thinking and feeling, even if they believe they do, and this type of clarification process can also help them to understand what is going on for them too. I am very good at communicating but I still do this all the time to make sure I have it right, and also as a tool to increase awareness of the athlete about what is going on for them. People often have what is called "compacted emotional experience" where a lot of thoughts and feelings are all stuck together making them difficult to work with if they are creating some type of block. In this case the communication needs to be expanded by breaking it down to understandable and manageable components.

While I was an instructor in teacher education at Michigan State, we often used an exercise where one person was given a simple message and that message was then whispered to another person who then gave it to another until it had gone all the way around the room. The last person would then say the message out loud and it was most often very distorted from the message given to the first person. This eye opening exercise pointed out that people often do not hear completely what is said to them or put their own spin on what they have heard, without their awareness. This is something you can do with a team if you want to emphasize the importance of accurate communication. It is usually pretty funny but emphasizes the importance of accurate communication.

With active listening, you can accomplish at least three important things:

1. You eventually get a clear unadulterated message from them unconfused by any thoughts, beliefs, perceptions or feelings you may hold.
2. When you state back to them what you heard, you verify that what you thought they said was what they meant to communicate, or not.
3. These responses send the nonverbal message that you care enough to try to understand their true experience and they feel a strong sense of support.

Exploratory Questions

When you check out the meaning of a communication and your athlete says that it's incorrect, or if you just need more information, you may want to go to an exploratory question. Exploratory questions, also called open-ended questions, help you gain more information without influencing the message coming to you. Exploratory questions do not furnish an answer, but generally help the athlete provide you with more accurate and complete information about their experience. You may get an "I don't know" but if you do not start offering them specifics and give them time to think about it, or ask other questions about what they want, think or feel, you will eventually get better information and establish healthy and effective communication. Generally, exploratory questions facilitate communication and feelings of being cared about. Non-exploratory or leading questions tend to obstruct communication and result in bad feelings and inaccurate information.

A guideline to think about exploratory questions is that they do not put words in the other person's mouth but instead gives them free rein to answer. The opposite of an exploratory question is a leading question which causes the athlete to focus on your thoughts and not theirs. For example if you say to your child "Are you sad?" they may answer yes or no. This is a leading question which focuses them on whether they are sad or not as opposed to helping them to identify what they feel. An alternative ques- tion could be "What are you feeling right now?" or "How did you feel when that happened?" They may give you an "I don't know." Resist the significant temptation to say "well do you feel ____." Be patient. You may ask them what they feel in their body, or pos- sibly have they ever felt that before in any other contexts. If you struggle to create exploratory questions it may help to think of them as "how" or "what" questions that never supply your athlete with a potential answer. An often useful exploratory question of simply asking if there is anything more will frequently help the athlete observe and communicate their experience more com- pletely. Whatever you do, do not tell the athlete they should not feel what they describe. Alternatively, look for the cause or, if necessary, look with them at the results of having the feeling and if the feeling creates problems. You can then look at processes which create more helpful feelings.

Honest Labeling

Labeling goes with paraphrasing as a response to a statement your child has made. In the active listening and exploratory questioning part of effective listening, we are trying to get the other person to tell us what their experience and perceptions are as they see them. After their statement, we respond with a statement that specifies what we heard them say to ascertain if what we heard is what they meant.

Honest labeling of a feeling or thought is going a little bit farther to make something concrete and can be the right thing to do when the athlete has finished specifying their experience to you. By labeling I mean identifying how the person is feeling, such as "You feel satisfied" or "You feel angry when it seems like I am not trying to help you" or "It sounds as if you feel confused", etc. You certainly do not want to do this prematurely while they are still sorting out their experience. When it appears clear they are saying a specific thing, honest labeling of what they are saying can provide the final accuracy check. You are looking for a response like "Yes Mom, that is what I mean" or "Yes, that is how I feel." The goal is to be able to tell the other person what you understand their communication to be and have them verify, "Yes that's it" or "no that's not it."

Honest labeling demonstrates not only that you are hearing what is being said, but also that you are willing to acknowledge it and accept it as their experience. This does not mean that you will support them continuing to do it, but only that you are willing to face that they are having the experience and are willing to deal with it. For example, no athlete wants to feel afraid, but opposed to hiding the feeling which offers little chance to change it, when they admit to you and them self that they are afraid, a solution can then be found. When a parent is listening effectively, the result is a complete and accurate understanding. The athlete feels understood and cared about and solutions can be pursued in an effective manner. There are far too many examples and situations to discuss them all here but if you follow the intent of the communication this process is somewhat self corrective and a lot of good things can be accomplished.

As an aside, these same communication skills can also be just as helpful in dealing with other parties to the sport experience such as coaches, members of the booster club and even the other parent. It is very common these days to find children with divorced parents. These communication skills can be tremendously helpful in forging the working relationship that is so important for the child to have as a base in this type of situation. Another aside, communication can be very complicated and if things keep getting stuck, I suggest getting some help. There are many good books of this fascinating subject. The old book by Eric Berne "The games that people play" offers excellent valuable insight into the complexity of communication, but there are many others.

Chapter 13

COMMUNICATING WITH YOUR COACH

Preparing to contact the coach

When communicating with your coach keep in mind one of the central concepts of this book, that of maintaining the correct balance, in this case between involvement and disengagement. An overly intrusive parent is one of the biggest problems coaches face, so don't be that parent that wastes valuable coach time and energy that is better spent working with the kids. Before you communicate with your coach take a moment to think through several factors that will influence the effectiveness of your communication. Ask yourself some of the relevant questions discussed below such as; "is this the right time, am I doing it in the right order, am I in an emotional state to effectively communicate, am I being fair or selfish, do I have the good information I need to proceed?" It is very important to communicate at the right time and about the right things, but it is at least equally important to avoid the reverse. Problematic communication with parents is the bane of all coaches and very costly in time and quality of the sport experience for the athlete. Do not take what I say as a suggestion to communicate or not in any specific situation, you have to make that decision, but the information and processes described in this chapter will make this important part of your child's experience easier and more effective for everyone concerned.

All coaches have an idea in their mind of how they want parents to work with them in order to create the most effective sport environment for their child. The nature of the optimal parent involvement varies between coaches and over different sport situations so you need to discover what is optimal in your situation. However, there is enough common to all situations that this review of positive communication factors may offer guidance in the right direction.

General considerations

To work well with the coach, you first have to communicate effectively with them. Here we are discussing communication opposed to talking to the coach, complaining to the coach, yelling at the coach or presenting a list of demands. You may remember a classic line from a movie where one character said "what we have here is a failure to communicate." You want an effective communication where emotions or other factors do not interfere with both parties fully understanding the message of the other person and a productive problem solving process results which creates the best solution possible at that time.

Over the years, I have found that most people think they are great communicators even when they are not. Some are better communicators than they think, but it is usually the other way around. Generally a poor communicator thinks they are a much better communicator than others perceive them to be. Additionally, it is common for the quality of communication to go down as the stress in a situation goes up. The point here, is to highlight the importance of monitoring the process of communication to make sure that the process remains effective until the question is resolved.

You as the parent need to take the responsibility to determine that desirable things are happening for your child. The challenge here is to determine what is desirable. I use the term challenge because this process is universally more complicated that it would appear and it is very important not to take the task lightly and reach a premature conclusion, one way or the other. No one is served and a lot of time can be lost by making a mountain out of a mole hill, but you need to do your due diligence. Although there are a lot of complicated factors that go into making the sport situation as desirable as possible, your reason for wishing to contact the coach may involve only one factor which may be resolved in a simple and straightforward communication with the right person.

It is important to start any communication by communicating respect for the other party by acknowledging good things you perceive such as their positive intent, behaviors, accomplishments and the like. If your emotions are running high, handle them in ways suggested here or however it works for you such that you are calm before you initiate a communication. If you are in a heightened emotional state before beginning communication, it will be more difficult for you to hear anything that runs counter to what you already believe to be true and the potential for misperception and emotional escalation increases on both sides. In fact, you should be or both end up on the same side, that of the child's best interest. But, if you are very distressed, or if you start by attacking the coach or administrator, resolving the question becomes much more difficult, which is in on one's interest. These days many coaches in organized programs are knowledgeable, highly skilled and have the welfare of the players as their first responsibility so if you start with an acceptance of this foundational belief, resolution of your concern should be reasonably easy.

Most coaches do good things, some better than others, and even good coaches may do some undesirable things. If you have a concern, you must act to resolve it. I do not mean instantly go on the warpath, this is easy for parents to do because their children are so important to them, but a calm and focused approach is a better way to start. The first step is the data gathering process described below which must be done effectively and includes beginning the process with an open mind. After the preliminary data gathering, if you still feel you have a legitimate need that is not being addressed, then it is necessary to pursue the question further. If you cannot gain an acceptable resolution with the coaching staff, then it is a reasonable option to begin going up the administrative ladder. If the situation is still unacceptable, then consider removing your child and finding a better situation. But, you must act wisely because the cost to everyone involved from bad decisions at this level could be significant.

Process of communication
Generally, the last place you want to inquire first is the administration. In a high school, for example, when parents go first to the principal or athletic director the process of resolving the question is significantly delayed. Everyone's time is wasted as the parent is generally directed to first deal with the individual with the most

relevant information, the coach. Although coaches differ regarding their preferences for communication, there is a logical order
that generally works best that can form a basis for your communication process.

We must start with understanding that most coaches in large
programs are extremely busy people. One high school football
coach I have worked with for 15 years gets up at 4 am every
morning and works non stop until he goes to sleep at 8 pm five
days a week all year, excepting game days when he might not get
to bed until after midnight. For reasons of efficiency and quality
it is important to a coach to have productive communication with
parents, but coaches differ somewhat in the process they believe
to be most effective. Although many of the suggestions in this
chapter are universally appreciated by coaches, it is important
to learn the specifics from your coach regarding how they want
the process to unfold. Most coaches will tell you this early in
the season, but if they do not, ask them and they will appreciate
the question. The communication skills discussed in the chapter
about communicating with your athlete all apply here, but the
additional guidelines offered in this chapter may help the process
be more efficient and productive.

When you need information or have a concern about something in the sport experience, there is a logical order of information gathering and communication that usually works best.
The first person you should talk to is usually your child athlete.
Remember the process discussed in the chapter about communicating with your athlete because you want good information from
them to start the inquiry process. Your athlete probably will have
very pertinent information that you don't have, which may go a

long way toward gathering the information you need to obtain a clear and complete understanding of the situation. I have seen parents rant at coaches for a lack of playing time when they did not know their child was resting from an injury or being held out for some other good purpose, such as being more rested for the next game.

If you still feel the need to talk to someone, then the next best person is usually the coach with the most contact with your child. In football, this might be the position coach. Continuing in the football example, the next choice might be the defense or offense coordinator and finally, the head coach. If a coach at any level cannot help you, or think your question needs to go higher, they will waste no time bumping you up to the next level.

Again, this is generally the process that works best. However, as the person ultimately responsible for your child, you need to assess and reassess the situation as it develops, including the communication procedure requested by the coach, and make your own choices.

Remember, you can be guaranteed that your coach wants to communicate with you about necessary information and wants to establish an optimal working relationship. You may be pleased or you may not be comfortable with what you think the coach is doing. You may have other concerns about the program, training, how your child is progressing, or where they are going and the like. It is critical that you address your concerns. However, it is just as critical that you do it in an effective manner. Effective communication, as stated earlier, will allow understanding to develop and not push anyone into feeling threatened or having to defend his or her position. This is a bigger issue than it might appear at first glance, so the importance cannot be overstated. Communicating in an open and non-threatening way will help you develop a trusting and effective relationship with the coach. Early successful interaction paves the way on several important dimensions for your child to be more successful. Supportive ways the coach may want you to be involved are discussed in the chapter on parent roles.

A large amount of information about procedures, goals and situations parents need to know is provided in booster club meetings. Attending those meetings is a good place to start gathering important information. Officers of the booster club and "team parents" may also be a source of basic information you need at the beginning of your data gathering process. Understanding the basic information is a critical beginning to developing the trusting and effective relationship with your coach that is so very important to your child.

Guidelines for the process

The following guidelines for communication with your coach may help you develop the effective working relationship that everyone wants and avoid misunderstandings, negative feelings and costly disruptions that will reduce the quality of the sport experience for everyone:

1. Remember, the coach is your hired expert. Although you may have played the sport in question or may have achieved great success in athletics or other areas, you are paying the coach to do a job. Communicate with them as needed and then step back and let them do their job. As

mentioned before, there are many important roles for parents, but being a sideline coach or constantly meddling in the training or competition is not one of them.

2. Show the coach you respect their position and expertise. When you give respect, you will get respect and this is a good start to having an effective working relationship.

3. Use effective communication skills. If communication is breaking down or you feel you have not been listened to, say so and work to resolve it. Communication skills discussed in the chapter on communicating with your athlete also apply to working with the coach, administration and other parents.

4. Show your coach that you appreciate the hard work and dedication they give to create the best sport experience possible. As a coach for many years, I can tell you that we appreciate it when parents show their appreciation for the hard work we are doing to create the intended outcome with their children.

5. Generally, it is useless to approach your coach about playing time. Please understand that, in a competitive rather than a participatory environment, coaches will play the child that they think will help them win. Most coaches will not keep a child from playing because they have some agenda against them, although many parents believe this is the case. Coaches will punish players by taking playing time away if necessary, only as a last resort. If you have questions about playing time, then explore the situation by following the normal sequence, including speaking with your child first. The main exception is that often coaches will put in less skilled players toward the end of a game if they are winning and the outcome

is not in jeopardy, so in this case the more skilled players may come out to give others a chance to participate. The only value in discussing playing time results if the coach can tell you some things your child can do to increase their playing time. Such things may include additional training time, individual coaching, extra workouts and the like.

6. Try to be objective and assess the situation realistically before contacting the coach about playing time or results. Many times, parents do not realize that although their child was a star in a small program, when they move into a much bigger program, they might be competing for playing time with a lot of other children that were stars in their original club or program. This is a very common occurrence which can sometimes be confusing for athletes as well as parents.

7. Do not think your child can do no wrong. Do not approach the coach in a biased way, thinking the coach must be doing something wrong or everything would be perfect for your little angel. For the welfare of your child, start the conversation with a belief that the coach is trying to do the best thing and foster an attitude of cooperation rather than confrontation. This is another very common situation that creates problems for athletes, parents and coaches.

8. Pick the right time to approach the coach. Just like talking to your child, it might seem most convenient for you to approach the coach right after practice or a game, but these are generally the worst times. Those are some of the busiest times for a coach and frequently the most charged with emotion, so not conducive to a specific and

well focused discussion. Even setting an appointment might be easier with a text or email sometime later when everyone has their schedule in front of them. Again, use your judgment because there are times, particularly after a win, that can be good times to briefly socialize and congratulate everyone for their good effort.

9. Seriously consider the 24 hour rule, where the parent will let 24 hours pass before contacting the coach, particularly when you are feeling the emotions of frustration or anger.

10. Think before you talk and gather pertinent information. It can be a long season and things can change during the year. Children may change and be different or they may be learning and changing at different rates than their peers. As always, gather information from your child first. Unnecessary emails or texts can be an additional burden for a coach. One high school basketball coach I worked with told me he would have 15 emails before he left the building after a game. He was an excellent coach and doing the right thing. Most of the emails were misguided time wasters where parents were trying to coach or complaining about playing time.

11. Remember to select carefully who you wish to speak with. A position coach will have more information about what your child needs to improve than the head coach. However, it all falls eventually or sometimes primarily on the head coach. If your questions are not answered, make an appointment to speak with the head coach at a mutually agreed upon time.

12. Try to follow the procedures requested by the coach when you seek to contact him. Email is good for information

exchange, but should not be used to discuss anything in any depth. If you need to talk to the coach, use email only to set up an appointment to speak on the phone or in person if the situation is not resolved easily with a call. Email messages are notorious for causing confusion and misunderstanding and should be used carefully.

13. Before contacting the coach for information, try other sources. See if the booster club has the information you seek and consider contacting the team parent, who often has additional information, or can serve as a good go-between for passing on information.

14. Remember to exercise professionalism when dealing with the coach. Approach the coach in a professional manner, like you would like to be approached in your job.

15. Observe yourself before communicating with the coach. Do not let impatience and emotion damage the working relationship with the coach.

16. Sometimes, the best thing to do is nothing. Other times, you need to act. Take the time to gather information and think about it for the right amount of time before contacting your coach.

17. In general, goals for the athlete and the year should be made known to you or be available upon request. This way, you will have an idea what the coach expects of your athlete and possibly understand better the sequence of events. If you cannot find this information in other sources, then a brief contact with the coach can serve to get everyone on the same page. This is an example where email could be the quickest method to gain information and additional clarification could be achieved with a quick phone call.

18. Remember, coaches are always looking for anything that will make their job easier and make their athletes more successful. Good communication and working effectively with parents is an important part of making this happen.

It is hoped that these guidelines will help you manage the important process of communication to most effectively support your coach and the athletic experience of your child. Some coaches are great but some may have behaviors or policies that are not good for your child. Remember, you do not know what your have until you gather sufficient information. The line between being an intrusive impediment to the sport program of your child, and intelligent oversight or support, may be a challenge to find. However, gathering necessary information in a stepwise fashion and taking wise action while being mindful of your impact on the process is a very important part of effectively supporting your child in sport.

Chapter 14
CHOOSING A SPORT

Timing

As you read this book, it is very likely that you child has already settled into one or more sports and the choice of sports has been made. Most athletes that excel in a sport devote an increasing amount of their time to that one sport as they grow older. As a child continues into high school, college, elite youth sports, professional or Olympic competition, this is how it needs to be, although many elite athletes have one or two other sports they engage in frequently.

However, at an early age it is a good idea to have child be involved in several sports. There are several important reasons to avoid overspecialization at too young an age. One obvious reason is that children cannot really know what sport they like the most until they have played several. At times children will gravitate toward a sport because someone they respect such as a parent or celebrity has played it. It may be the best sport for them but it is important to keep in mind their motivation for choosing a sport because this is a frequent cause of many undesirable effects resulting from a mismatch of athlete to sport. In this case, you may want to let them try it, but you may also want to insist that they try some other sports that might be fun and possibly a better match for their resources. This gives them an opportunity to see what they like and there is plenty of time for specialization later. Frequently I see junior tennis players that have been playing since they were four years old. But, I also often see other juniors who are equally as good, and may go just as far, that may have only started two years before I meet them.

Cross training

A great amount of information has recently emerged relating over use injuries and uneven physical development to early specialization. Cross training with several sports can help by reducing the repetitive motion and specific physical stresses characteristic to a single sport while strengthening the body in different ways. Other sports may simply provide something that is fun or may provide a counter point such as swimming which is a very different experience and uses the body very differently than soccer.

Although it may seem at first glance that it would not make a difference, it does matter which sports are included in a cross training program. Generally all sports should be fun but there may be some things to consider in the choice of one over another. Some sports compliment the demands of other sports such as sprinting in track might be of value in producing speed for football. On the other hand, some sports that seem logically complementary can even be counter productive. For example over the years many tennis and other coaches have instructed players to run distance to create endurance, which is clearly needed in a long match. But recent research and experience has found that the slow pace of distance running makes a player significantly slower on the court. For this reason when considering components of the sport selected for additional training, it is important to evaluate the task demands of the additional sport for a good match. Additionally, it is a good idea to evaluate their other activities for components that may detract from performance in some way.

Recent development in training has included sport specific training where the same motion that is used in a sport is isolated and specifically trained. A good example is weight training a movement of the arm that is used in a tennis swing. It is correct that that type of training often does help in the sport, but the risk of over training is realistic in this type of cross training and must be carefully guarded against with young athletes.

Evaluating sport specific factors

It is of importance to all parents and athletes to realistically evaluate the physical demands and risks that vary between sports. Football and tennis are both very physically demanding but put a premium on a different type of physical development and pose different physical risk factors. Golf, which is very demanding of physical precision and mental focus, also can create an injury but of a very different nature than football. Cheerleading which was thought of as safe and maybe not even considered a sport, is now high on the list of serious injuries with the introduction of more gymnastic tricks and tumbling.

There are a number of factors you may wish to consider in the nature of the experience your child will encounter. Not only the task demands but also aspects of the environment in which the sport is based need to match the interest of your child.

For instance combat sports such as martial arts, wrestling and football create a different atmosphere than many other sports. The motive to defeat another person, also know as the need for power, is prominent in the combat and contact sports, where it is less so in others. One athlete decided to leave martial arts when he decided he did not want to feel the aggressive feelings that were necessary to be effective in that sport and instead satisfied his motivations for physical activity and thrills, but without the aggression and hostility, in mountain climbing. Recall in our discussion of motivation that there are many different motivations for being involved in sports so it can be quite important to match the individual constellation of motivation and needs of your child as much as possible. Sometimes athletes feel the need to participate in more than one sport to get what they need.

While parents and kids are exploring different sports, factors such as the availability of opportunity to engage in the sport and the cost of equipment are sometimes not taken into consideration initially, but can become a burden later. It is pretty easy to find a place to play tennis, the equipment is not real expensive, but you still have to get someone to play with. Cycling is pretty easy for most to engage in as it is an individual sport and places to ride can be easily available, but the costs of equipment can be quite high. Running is the easiest where all you need is a pair of shoes. Rowing on the other hand may require significant travel time to water for most people and an expensive boat. Frequently several sports may be equally satisfactory to an athlete so sometimes it is a good idea to entertain multiple options in the beginning and be supportive if your athlete feels a need to narrow down their activity or change to another sport as time goes on.

Team vs. individual sport considerations

Another important choice for the parent and athlete is that of a team or individual sport. Remembering from the discussion on motivation it is important for the desire to be part of a team or the lack of this desire to be addressed in deciding on a sport. The desire to be part of a team, to experience belonging to something and the experience of cooperation in working toward a common goal is enormously important to some athletes. Other athletes do not want the many complicating factors that arise when others are involved and want to exclusively focus on their own game. Neither is better, but frequently athletes with a mismatch on this factor experience continual frustration. This all would seem obvious as we sit here and think about it, but all too often kids go blindly into a sport that is not conducive to satisfaction of their primary motivations. Not matching motivation is one of the biggest reasons kids will be unhappy in a sport and do more poorly as a result.

Monitoring their experience

I mentioned earlier that kids tend frequently wish to enter a sport that someone important to them participated in such as a sports hero, parent or a sibling. This type of choice can also be promoted by the parent at a conscious or unconscious level. It is important for you to be mindful of the potential for this to happen and act appropriately. It might be the best primary sport for the child, or not, but a stepwise evaluation of needs and motivations followed by having the child participate in several options will usually lead in the direction of a good choice.

Many children change sports, even through their high school years. This is common and although it may not fit a parent fantasy of the child developing high skill in one sport, it might be what a child needs. It is important to be mindful of the things you want from the participation of your child in sport and evaluate periodically how you feel about their sport activity. Being aware of your feelings will help you be sure that you are not confusing your wants and needs with those of your child. Talking in a casual and relaxed manner with them about their feelings regarding different sports and what they are looking for from the sport can keep you informed of their experience and identify questions you need to pursue to make sure they are having the experience you both want.

Chapter 15

CHOOSING A COACH AND CLUB

Choosing the right environment

Once it has been decided that your child is going to participate in a sport, there are often some choices of a coach, club program and facility. If your child is already in a sport and club, some of the considerations reviewed here may help your evaluate the quality of the situation. There are ranges of good to bad on many dimensions in your child's sport experience and making a good choice can have an enormous impact on how healthy and valuable your child's experience will be. The implications are significant because children learn many lessons in sports that are carried forth as an operational format to many areas of their life. The lessons learned in sports can have a huge impact on their future success and happiness. In fact, this is one of the reasons many parents want their kids to be involved in a sport. The lessons include but are not limited to developing an appreciation for fitness, creating a strong and healthy body, creating a good work ethic, learning how to apply themselves to a challenge and learning how to work cooperatively with others.

Now, it is true that your child may already be in a sport where the situation is set and you may not be able to make some of these decisions. They may be in a school sports program and what is there is mainly what you get. But even in the most rigid programs you may be able to exert some influence that can increase the value of their sport experience. For instance in a high school football program there may be little you can do to influence the program, and intrusions that disrupt a program are usually not appreciated, but you may find information here that could help your child operate more effectively in the situation.

It is of utmost importance to have your child in an environment where they have the best chance to be successful. But success can be defined in many ways. Recall that we discussed that there are a wide range of motivations and reasons an athlete may want to be in a sport. Some of these motivations are more naturally available in certain sports. We have previously discussed the impact that choice of sport can have, but the opportunity to achieve success, or we might say satisfaction of a motivation, can also be strongly influenced by the coach and specifics of the environment.

The value of choosing an environment that fits with the needs, motivations and abilities of your child and being with a coach who brings the combination of values, knowledge, goals, procedures and interpersonal skills that are right for your child cannot be underestimated. Of course this is not a perfect world and the perfect coach and environment may not be available. You may wish to start with prioritizing the environment and coaching factors important to you, and your child, and investigate the range of situations where the highest priority needs can be satisfied.

In younger age groups some of the more important factors usually include level of participation, level of competition pressure, the way the athletes are treated and the overall fun in the atmosphere the coach helps create. At younger levels the goals of most good coaches focus more toward teaching and athletic development. Young athletes just want to have fun and when they have fun, they will want to do more of it. Competition is usually minimized in younger age programs, but there are a few who bring more difficult training and competition in at an earlier time.

Competition vs. participation environment

One important choice you need to make is whether to have your child involved in a participation or competition environment. Competition environments emphasize playing well and winning where participation environments emphasize playing time. Participation environments are more consistently found across the board in younger age groups. As we have discussed, there are many potential drawbacks associated with competition when it is not handled well, particularly in younger age groups. Remember our discussion about how introduction of too much emphasis on competition too early will frequently turn a child off to sports in general.

This concept is often ignored but is important to consider and correctly match the ratio of competition vs. participation to the needs of your child. In one very successful high school sports team, some parents became very angry because their senior children did not get as much playing time as they wished. They directed their anger at the coach in ways that resulted in damaging the quality of the experience for everyone. In this situation, the team had just moved up to a tougher division and was playing teams that brought significantly greater resources and the coach was playing the kids that he thought would give the team the best chance to win. Two of ten games were decided by one play. If the coach had played the less skilled players, the margin would not have been as close and the team would not have had a chance to win several of the games. At times, when the team was significantly ahead, the coach would play anybody that had a uniform on, but when it was close everyone expected him to do his best to win in the competitive situation, and that's what he did. It is not known whether the parents had talked to their kids first to gather information, or if they just did not understand the difference between competitive and cooperate situations, or if they just did not care, but the parents were on the wrong footing and were destructive to the environment. Even in the competitive situation the team members that did not play in the games still had an important role on the team, but for reasons unknown this was not enough for the parents. Do not just gloss over this concept. Although most parents do not think about this concept, matching the correct environment to the current needs of your child may have a significant impact in a number of ways.

Matching skill and level of challenge

In many upper level teams, there are those athletes that do not get as much playing time as they would at a lower level of competition. At the higher level the emphasis is always on winning. Generally for an early developmental player this would not be the ideal environment regarding playing time. However, there are a few reasons that a younger and less skilled player might want to spend some time on a team like this. Notice I said some time. Younger athletes can sometimes learn a lot from watching more highly skilled players who can serve as models for a number of different things. In this type of situation older players can model many things such as a good work ethic, dedication, exerting strong effort, leadership, trustworthiness, support for other team members and high level skill performance. At times it may be valuable for your athlete to practice with kids with higher level skills but at other times, it may be of greater value to practice and play with kids of the same level. It depends on what your child needs at the time but as we previously discussed, most of the time usually needs to be spent by young players in participation where they can spend substantial time developing their skills and enjoying the experience.

Generally, the ideal level of challenge is where the athlete can obtain some success whether in their own advancement or against competitors. If the competition or training level is too high or too low the athlete may become discouraged, develop bad habits, reduce their level of achievement and may even quit whether they actually leave the sport or not. It is necessary for the athlete to derive inner reinforcement from something, whether it is being a member of a highly skilled and successful team, seeing improvement in their skill level or even winning competitions. The trick is to know what is most important for your athlete at a specific time and then be able to access it if possible.

Individual vs. team sports
Youth sports is a valuable environment for children to cultivate personal attributes and interpersonal skills. In the individual sports the emphasis is on individual development with interpersonal skill development mostly limited to sportsmanship and working with the coach. The team sports are a fertile ground to develop social skills such as communication, cooperation and

other skills important to teamwork. Some parents have chosen to have their child in team sports just to achieve these goals because many times there are so few opportunities, particularly with home schooling, elsewhere for this experience. Early in their sports career I suggest exposing your child to a variety of sports that may fit their motivation and attempt to create some balance between team and individual sports. As your child develops it will become more clear where to emphasize sports activity if you maintain good communication with them about their experience.

Age, size and personality

Youth programs are doing a much better job matching age and size in their programs these days. Still, it is important for you to monitor this situation to make sure your child is in an environment that minimizes risk from mismatch of age, size and ability.

It is the same thing for personality considerations. I worked with an athlete who was a great kid with significant talent in soccer. Unfortunately, he was on a team where some kids were bigger and had bad attitudes. One kid who was a leader was demeaning, hostile and negative. He was also a wrestler who, according to my client, "could beat everybody else up." The wrestler would self limit his success because of his bad attitude but he also created an environment that was harmful to the success of several other players on the team. My client said he did not dare to give the bully feedback because he did not want to get beaten up. I told the father about the problem and suggested he talk to the father of the bully and coach. He came back saying the father of the bully denied any problem and that the coach did not want to deal with it. Maybe the coach was afraid of the father of the bully or maybe he was afraid of losing a good player because this was a competition oriented team, the reason is unknown. Whatever his reason, I think it was the wrong decision for the coach to not confront the situation and demand change in the player's behavior. Even in a competitive situation I believe there are some things that must not be sacrificed for the sake of a win. I suggested the father consider the costs and benefits of moving his son to a different team. Most good coaches of younger athletes that I know would demand a change in player behavior or he would be off the team. It is my opinion that there is never a place for a bully on a team and that the situation should be rectified, one way or another.

Facility and safety considerations

An important consideration for the parent is the facility the athlete will use. A good facility will address and attend to safety issues and maintain equipment in good working order. When you are choosing a club or facility, observing and inquiring about the quality and condition of the facility is of significant importance.

Be careful about assuming that safety needs are satisfied. Take a good look both at the physical facility and the availability of safety or emergency resources. Everyone knows now of the importance of water in the heat but also take some time to think about other things your child will encounter. A tennis coach was having kids run in a nearby grass field for conditioning. One of the athletes stepped in a hole that could not be seen and fractured her back which created a world of trouble for her. This athlete was in excellent condition, the blame was entirely on the coach for having them run in a dangerous environment. It is almost impossible for the parent to evaluate everything and they trusted the coach to be safe when he obviously was not up to the task.

It is a challenge for parents to adequately oversee everything and a perfect situation or coach may not be available. The important thing is for you to look at the situation and make an informed analysis regarding the venue, equipment and coach activities to make sure safety considerations are within limits you find appropriate. Do not try to act in a vacuum. Gather information from several sources, talk to other parents, and if you have a concern talk to the coach. Most of the time a good solution can be found.

Additional Coaching Considerations
Coaches come in all variations. Not one is alike, but many of them share a significant number of attributes, both good and bad. Depending on your situation, the coach may be a parent volunteer or they may have elite accreditation with years of experience and success. It is important to understand who the coach is to make sure they are a match for your athlete and to ascertain the best way in which to work with them.

Regardless of the level of the coach it is important that they create a physically and emotionally healthy experience for your athlete. There have been many books and courses made available addressing how this is best accomplished by the coach and what parents should be looking for. Some important duties of a good coach are; making sure equipment and other physical needs are dealt with appropriately, incorporating drills which are physically safe with technique appropriate for the level of your child, and having the goals and attitude of the coach coincide with the needs of your athlete.

Unfortunately, it has frequently been the case in the past that the coaches that taught beginning or lower level players were often the least well trained and at times taught wrong techniques that needed to be fixed later. It is worth the time to find the most qualified coach possible. Although you may have a great coach, no coach can be everything to everybody. It also may be worthwhile to seriously consider obtaining some extra coaching on technique from a coach you know to be very skilled to get your athlete off to a good start. I consider this very good money spent, the old adage "a stitch in time saves nine" could not be truer than it is here.

The same is true for mental skills as for the physical skills specific to the sport. The sharpest coaches on the mental game that I have encountered were also those most knowledgeable in the role of sport psychology. As I briefly mention in another part of the book, one Division 1 coach I worked with had taken a class in sport psychology in college. We worked together with the team seamlessly and the team tied for third in the NCAA. Despite my pleas that we were poised to win it all the next year, the coach resigned with comments such that "she had not lived with her husband for several years because he worked in another state and that she needed have a family life." Although I am 100% committed to helping athletes compete at their best, I had to admit that she had a point. The coach left with the assurance to me and the team that the next coach would use me again.

For some reason the next coach apparently thought she knew more than the preceding coach about sport psychology, with the lack of credentials that usually accompanies ignorance by the way, paid only lip service to using me, and the same team that had previously tied for third at nationals, with more experience, finished way down in the rankings after she took the helm. It is unknown what unworthy motive for not providing sport psychology to the team the coach was engaged in, but the kids were the ones who paid the big price by missing out on one of their few opportunities to do well in the NCAA. It was hard to see the team members in the hallway that I knew so well from the year before and hear their sadness, disappointment and frustration that I had not been made available to them. Not surprisingly, the students also paid a long term price because, due to the poor performance, scholarships for that team were cut by the athletic director. In contrast, the much more knowledgeable previous coach had brought the team to unprecedented prominence through success, which had been rewarded with respect and an increase in scholarships. As they say, "ignorance has it's price."

For reasons unknown many coaches think it is a good idea to experiment with an idea they got from someone or a book in sport psychology and just see how it works. Why they think it is ok to "experiment" with the progress of their athletes is a mystery to me. These coaches appear to not have even a clue that that they are robbing their athletes of the opportunity to learn extremely valuable mental skills from a qualified professional. The reason more coaches do not embrace professional sport psychology is currently unknown. It does not seem logical and is clearly seen to be counterproductive by those that understand the situation. One explanation might be that research on the mind has found that humans tend to have a tremendous difficulty literally seeing something that they have no schema for, or that they believe does not exist. I often wonder at the frequent amazement of coaches when they see the improvements of athletes after learning mental skills. My answer, although I do not say this to them, is "well what did you expect?" Although they were intelligent enough to include mental training, apparently they still did not realize the dramatic impact it could have. As we have said before, the mind operates mechanically and any time you learn to use any machine more efficiently, such as your smart phone, a computer or your automobile, you will get better results. It only seems logical to expect the athletes to hit new personal records, which is consistently the outcome. I never expect anything less.

However, whether the coach mistakenly thinks they are qualified to teach the sport psychology an athlete needs, or does not include professional mental training based on a lack of knowledge, lack of openness to new information, fear of losing control or not appearing to know everything, turf issues, or some other reason, the negative impact on your child is the same. If you have a coach like this, good luck helping them realize that they just might not know as much as they think they know. That may be impossible, but it is worth a well crafted attempt. You may remember a famous line from a movie that applies here where the character, Detective Harry Callahan, said of a criminal he had just apprehended, "a man's got to know his limitations." I have been very involved in many sports for many years and know a great deal about several sports, but I also respect my limitations and know enough to understand that this knowledge does not make me qualified to be a coach in any of those sports. Even in tennis, golf and football, in which I have played and competed extensively, I always defer technique and operational questions back to the coach, and your sport psychologist should do the same. Ideally, your coach would also understand their limitations regarding making professional quality knowledge of the mental game available to your athlete. If not, the responsibility falls on you to make knowledge of the mental game available to your child that will give them the best chance of reaching their potential.

A coach not knowing their limitations can create less of a winning season for them self, but the effect of not providing your athlete with tools they can use to have a better sport experience can have a much larger short and long term impact on them. This is a very unfortunate situation because I have seen many teams under perform and the players experience losses and sadness that were totally unnecessary, only because the players made wrong choices on what to think where the right choices could have been just as easily made after one session of the Essential Concepts Mental Training Program. Eventually, in the future, all coaches will welcome the services of a Sport Psychologist just as any good coach now embraces weight training, nutrition and safety issues. It is just unknown when the general awareness of sport psychology will reach the level of these other adjuncts to performance. All coaches at the highest, Olympic, level currently embrace sport psychology and would consider it ridiculous for an athlete to not be trained in mental skills. I argue that it is just as important to the younger athlete to know how to train and compete most effectively.

It is not reasonable for you to expect your coach to be competent in sport psychology. Sport psychology is a very technical field requiring significant background to be competent. This is discussed more completely in the chapter on choosing a sport psychologist. Many intelligent coaches that value sport psychology still believe it is only for athletes who are having some performance problem. Although it is true that some clinical sport psychologists can help athletes with performance issues, that is not the main value of sport psychology. The main value of sport psychology, specifically mental training, is that it provides knowledge that every athlete can use to be more effective. One of the most famous head coaches of a professional team that I have worked with acknowledged that he did not understand what I was doing, but employed me because he knew all his athletes would become better. If an athlete started having performances issues, he would send them to me and I would get them back on track, but that was not my main purpose with the team.

There are going to be many differences in coaching philosophies regarding running a team or in coaching individuals. Several philosophies may be equally correct or have equal value. One of the challenges you face as a parent is to understand and evaluate the relative value of the philosophies in coaches your child will encounter. What is already known is not necessarily the best, but newer is not always better either. It may be of value to take the time to think through philosophies and orientations of coaches as they relate to your child's best interest.

Coaches display the full range of personalities. It is best to match your athlete with a coach who can support their development and reflect personality qualities and values you feel are appropriate. Coaches are seen by athletes as surrogate parents and have a huge impact on them. On private teams, the athlete may be with the coach four hours a day, which is more interactive time than parents normally get. Mainly it is important to make sure the coach respects the athletes and deals with them appropriately. To deal with your athlete appropriately, it is important for the coach to understand them. If you sense a lack of communication, we suggest you approach the coach with your concern at an appropriate time and open up a discussion about your concerns or questions.

First and foremost, you should never place your child with a coach, no matter how good their reputation, where the coach thinks they need to intimidate or abuse the child for any reason. Nothing is worth subjecting your child to this type of behavior. This creates significant problems for the child, now as well as in the future. There should be an overriding atmosphere of respect and sensitivity. This does not mean the coach cannot be tough and push the athlete if needed, but it needs to be done right.

I once worked with a young soccer player that was a gifted athlete with a great attitude in competition. But, after working with a new coach for awhile, his attitude changed significantly and he lost his joyful and self directed great competition mind-set, changing to one of self distrust, low esteem, fearfulness, and competition anxiety. I believe the coach was one of the pros that played well but had no clue how to coach another athlete in a healthy positive manner. So let me make it clear, just because a coach was a great athlete that does not mean they are a good or even healthy coach. Playing and coaching are two different skill sets. There are good and bad coaches at all levels, your challenge is to first make sure the coach is not destructive and then secondly find the type of coach that can guide your athlete to their highest and best.

Most coaches, when approached in a respectful manner, are happy to talk and are eager to reach greater understanding which may solve problems and make the parent a more effective member of the whole team effort. If you have a concern, then it is important to approach the coach with your questions in a respectful and timely manner. Unless there is a clear danger, it is almost never appropriate for a parent to initiate a communication with a coach during a competition or practice. The important thing is to have a meaningful communication with the coach at some point about the topic, leading to a plan and situation that makes sense to you.

On the other hand, this does not mean that the parent should try to control all aspects of the situation to their liking. Over interference by the parent is not welcomed by any coach and it uniformly results in a great many additional problems which take away from the ideal environment for the athlete. With the variables under discussion here, as with others we have discussed, do not assume you have the right answer just because that is what you think. Although you may be extremely busy like many other parents, taking the time to work through the information and your feelings with an open mind may result in a situation that is significantly more valuable for your child.

There are many sources that address effective coaching. A majority of coaches beyond the level of parent assistants frequently attend seminars addressing the many different aspects of coaching. You can also access a lot of this information which may help you think about your questions before you contact the coach. If you think danger is imminent, then you must act immediately, if not, then there is probably time for you to do a little research. As we have discussed before, when parents approach a coach at an appropriate time with a pleasant attitude, most coaches will be happy to discuss their concerns, and frequently an increase in value for the child will result.

Chapter 16

CHOOSING A SPORT PSYCHOLOGIST

The challenge

As a parent of an athlete you may have noticed that the amount of knowledge, goods and services available to you that are supposed to help your athlete compete more effectively has grown exponentially. The offerings can seem endless whether it involves extra coaching, extra physical training, nutritional knowledge and supplements, the latest equipment and even training aids and gadgets. The fact is that advancements have been made in many areas which can make a real difference in safety and performance, but sorting through the maze to find the value can be a real challenge.

Unfortunately the same thing is true for sport psychology services but the maze is even much more complex. Parents are bombarded with infomercials, specials on sports channels, flyers and information provided through coaches. Parents are presented with an increasingly large number of individuals offering a wide range of services ostensibly dealing with technical mental operations in an area of knowledge with which most people who are not psychologists are unfamiliar. The somewhat esoteric nature of the material makes it very difficult for a parent to evaluate the value of the offering as well as the capability of the person wishing to provide services.

This is unfortunate because a set of well developed mental skills is critical for your athlete to avoid mental mistakes that may seem reasonable choices to make, but are actually damaging, and to understand how to use their mind so they can make the most of their resources. You may recall from earlier in the book our discussion of the performance triad, which also includes a physical ability component and sport specific knowledge and skills. All the best coaches and athletes now know that, at any level, an athlete with adequate sport psychology knowledge has a decided advantage over one without them. These days practically every champion talks about the importance of their mental game in the post competition interview and that their ability to focus made the difference. It is my hope that the discussion of the following concepts will give you a useful framework to evaluate the overall competency and specific abilities of a provider in order to find the right match for your child. Please do not believe that just because someone is offering services and may have credentials, or look good on paper, that they are competent to provide good services and not create new problems. That is simply not true. But there are a lot of competent providers who can give your child the training they need, you just have to find them.

We can begin the process of separating the good from the bad with a review of the professional background and skills that are needed to competently provide sport psychology services.

Background basis for competency

To competently provide sport psychology services I believe at least minimal standards in several areas must be met. Although all athletes need to possess the basic knowledge of how their mind works, each athlete is different to some extent in their mental training needs. In addition, all providers are somewhat different in level of psychological knowledge, type of training, background knowledge in sport psychology and experience, so do not be surprised if you have to review several programs or interview several providers to find a good match.

It is my opinion that anyone offering any type of sport psychology services, including mental training, must have a professional knowledge of psychology. The mind is very complicated and although some teaching of concepts can be done without a professional level of psychological knowledge, to effectively help an athlete make specific changes or even adapt the basic information to their specific needs, usually requires an advanced level of psychological knowledge and skills. Sufficient background knowledge in the field of sport psychology is also essential. Training as a Clinical Psychologist does not qualify someone to be a sport psychologist.

However, providers that can offer mental training of irreplaceable value and good books are available. The following review of the categories of sport psychology service providers is a good place to begin reviewing key factors you can use to evaluate programs and providers.

Clinical Sport Psychology

The most highly trained provider is the Clinical Sport Psychologist (CSP). Although great Clinical Sport Psychologists such as

Dr. Bruce Ogelvie, Dr. Jim Loehr, Dr. Albert Rodinov of the USSR and Dr. Lahrs-Eric Usenthal of Sweden were working before this time, this designation became more widely known as a result of the USOC program which sought to identify qualified providers for work with US Olympic athletes. To be a CSP one must first be a trained clinical or counseling psychologist. In practice clinical and counseling psychologists are indistinguishable and so in our discussion they will be lumped together under the term of clinical psychologists. A person can be a good CSP without being on the USOC registry, but to be on the registry and work with Olympic athletes the CSP must pass stringent USOC requirements including hundreds of hours working with elite athletes and coaches. When I joined the USOC in 1985 there were only about 10 other CSP certified to be on the registry.

To be a Clinical Psychologist one must first have a Ph.D., Psy.D. or a qualifying Ed.D. This degree requires at least four years of graduate education in an APA approved school to cover the basic knowledge of psychology. The education might include a two year master's degree plus at least another two years of class work during the doctoral study, or it may be done without a masters degree. For example, my program included a M.A. in Human Learning and Development followed by the doctoral work in Counseling, Clinical and Mind Body Psychology, but there are many variations that are sufficient to provide basic knowledge.

After course work a Clinical Psychologist must then receive supervised practice in working with clients seeking services in the clinical setting which is followed by an internship of supervised practice. The internship is critical to develop safe and effective skills for working with people and usually lasts for a year.

To practice as a Psychologist, or even call oneself a Psychologist in most states, the individual must have come from an APA approved program, APA approved internship, pass an extremely rigorous national exam and be licensed by a state examining board. To maintain the license to practice the Psychologist must satisfy a continuing education requirement. Being licensed as a Clinical Psychologist does not necessarily mean the individual is a good or effective clinician, it simply means they have met certain minimal educational and practice qualifications to be licensed and practice.

There is no separate licensing for a sport psychologist. When I began working in the field in 1974 there was no separate field of sport psychology in the United States and no accreditation. The number of people doing research or working with sport psychology in the US at that time could be easily counted on both hands. In 1985 I was a founding member of the United States Association of Applied Sport Psychology (AASP). AASP later developed criteria for education of sport psychologists and a certification they call a Sport Psychology Consultant. It is not necessary in AASP to have the rigorous training of a licensed psychologist, although some do, so AASP does not identify people in their program as "Psychologists" but as "Consultants." The only quality control at this time for licensed psychologists who wish to call themselves sport psychologists is that they are expected to satisfy specific ethical guidelines that demand competency, but there are no specific training requirements, adherence is voluntary and competency is far from assured. AASP certification does require some sport psychology training, and has required more over the years, but still does not demand consultants to be licensed clinical psychologists and it is important to note that although AASP certification does indicate a specific amount of training in Sport Psychology, it does not necessarily guarantee competency either.

As a footnote, Sport Psychiatrists are medical doctors who have taken specific training in psychiatry and usually some education in sport psychology. Generally, Psychiatrists treat symptoms with medication and do not engage in psychotherapy which can be defined as attempting to help a person change by talking to them and changing the way they think. Some Psychiatrists engage in variable amounts of psychotherapy up to the extreme end where the most highly trained group, Psychoanalysts, seek cure through long term intensive psychotherapy. I have a partner who is a Sport Psychiatrist who refers all clinical sport psychology requests to me. At times athletes have a need for medication to deal with some psychiatric symptoms and a sport psychiatrist should be more on top of what medications will interfere with play or be on a banned list and inappropriate for athletes at higher levels.

There are some masters level counselors that have a background which includes clinical training, supervised experience and significant sport psychology knowledge. Some individuals from this group are quite competent and can have something valuable to offer. Some masters level individuals are more effective than some psychologists. However, in some psychologically complicated situations, or when a solution cannot seem to be found, the more extensive training of a Clinical Psychologist may be productive of a solution.

Adequate professional psychology knowledge and clinical training are necessary but not sufficient. Significant sport psychology background knowledge is also necessary but not sufficient to provide helpful services. Too many psychologists think because they ran track, read a book or went to a few classes that this qualifies them to be a sport psychologist, which is an egregious error. The knowledge base in Sport Psychology has grown over the years from minimal to a fairly large amount of very specific information. To provide competent services, a provider really needs to be well versed in both professional and sport psychology. Any provider will come to you with some background in training and knowledge they believe is relevant but remember having a background, no matter how extensive, does not equal competency. I know some Masters level Sport Psychologists that are more successful in providing services than some licensed Clinical Sport Psychologists, so the individual differences in ability between providers does make a difference.

Educational Sport Psychology
The USOC also has a category for providers labeled Educational Sport Psychologists. They identified this group as capable of providing educational experiences but not qualified, due to lack of clinical training, to work with athletes who had significant performance issues. Although they probably will not be labeled as such, most mental training programs fall into the category of Educational Sport Psychology.

Individuals who are not clinicians can still provide good educational programs. When using them you just need to be aware of their limitations. In addition to not recognizing more complicated psychological issues or solutions to an issue, many providers who are not licensed clinical psychologists do not have the obligation to adhere to the Ethical Guidelines of Psychologists, which can lead to problems. A few years ago a person doing educational sport psychology work for a professional team found that they could not help a pitcher who had chronic problems with a slump. Because the provider was not a clinician he was not bound by and possibly not aware that the Ethical Code for Psychologists demands that a psychologist refer someone they cannot help to someone else who can. The pitcher was not referred and after spending time with several teams, but never able to escape from the slump, retired with an unsuccessful career when he could have been easily helped by a Clinical Sport Psychologist with the necessary skills.

Certified Hypnotherapists

A group that deserves mention identifies itself as Certified Hypnotists. Individuals in this group frequently will offer hypnosis as a method to accomplish all sorts of goals such as increased performance, reduced performance anxiety and even escape from slumps. Although some psychologists use hypnosis, certified hypnotists are not trained psychologists. Their training is created and supervised by themselves with no accountability to the American Psychological Association, the psychologists code of ethics or other professional psychology criteria. The amount of psychology education required for certification as a hypnotist is often unknown and without detailed review and analysis may be properly considered as nonexistent. Hypnosis can be a valuable tool in the hands of a qualified Clinical Psychologist, but it is only a tool that must be integrated into a treatment program based upon a highly developed level of professional and clinical psychology knowledge. If you consider working with a hypnotist, I suggest reviewing their background for presence of the psychological training criteria I have discussed above as basic competency to work with another person.

I have researched and taught hypnosis for many years. When I became interested in hypnosis during graduate school my wise advisor, Dr. Norman Kagan, told me "the important thing about hypnosis is not to be able to hypnotize someone, but to understand what it can tell us about how the mind works." Subsequently, I have used my understanding of mental operations gained from the study of medical hypnosis, human learning and Neurolinguistic Programming (NLP) to help athletes learn to operate their mind more efficiently for over 35 years. Most hypnotists think they can hypnotize an athlete to do what the athlete wants and that is all there is to it. Although there may be exceptions, I have not seen any certified hypnotist training that met the standards I reviewed above in professional and sport psychology, and I consider most of them as having the potential for harmful effects. Some athletes may have been helped by them, but over the years I have worked with many athletes who have been confused, had their precious time wasted or been literally set back in their progress by hypnotists, as well as other providers, that did not know what they were doing.

Other providers
The other group of providers consists of coaches, athletes who have played professionally and individuals from other fields who think they have valuable information for athletes. Some retired players have good insights that can be useful to other athletes. I often tell athletes in lectures that they are lucky that I was not an Olympic or professional athlete because my program would be about what I learned and how I did it. This is usually the nature of

mental training programs provided by former athletes, and if they were successful, they usually have some good advice. The difference in the mental training program described in this book is that it is the result of an analysis of the mental skills used by hundreds of athletes to win major championships. Providers from other fields can have very useful things to teach athletes, but you just need to look at the substance of the particular program, decide if it addresses your child's needs, and determine if the provider satisfies your criteria for someone to influence your child.

Coaches as sport psychologists

These days any competent coach has a healthy appreciation for the role of the mind in sports. I often refer to coaches as the first sport psychologists because the mind has always been a key factor in sports and they were the only one standing there. Most coaches who receive any qualifying or continuing education are exposed to some knowledge of sport psychology. Unfortunately, many of them fail to understand that this minimal exposure is not sufficient to make them a sport psychologist. The old saying that false knowledge is more dangerous than expressed ignorance, is nowhere more true than here. In the same way, from having worked with sports for over 35 years I have learned quite a bit about many sports, but I know enough to respect my limitations and realize that this knowledge does not make me a qualified coach in any of them.

You must not depend blindly on your coach to sufficiently address the mental game. Coaches fail to include mental training from sport psychology providers for a number of reasons. It has been suggested that these reasons include ignorance of the value it can bring, fear of losing control of their team, fear of interference by the sport psychologist in team operations, or even fear that parents will believe that the coach should know this material or that the coach believes that the children are mentally ill or otherwise inadequate. None of this is true, but at this point, the basis of coaches concerns is all conjecture. I currently have a research project underway to determine the answer.

My belief is that attitudes and beliefs change slowly and despite clear evidence that mental training increases performance, coaches still have a hard time believing that it can help their athletes be successful. This may be the reason that I have found that the coaches more knowledgeable in sport psychology are those who more quickly include sport psychology in their training programs. For this reason you must not depend on your coach, but must take the responsibility yourself, to make sure your child has the mental tools they need to train and compete most effectively. Many parents have expressed frustration that, although their child was performing at a very high level after mental training, the rest of the team of which they were a member, was not. In these cases the coach was not providing mental training to the rest of the team which held down the potential for successful competitions.

In speaking with some coaches it has become clear to me that, although they were good coaches and wanted nothing more than great performance, coaches generally did not know what mental training actually was. It followed that they did not know how mental training could fit in with the rest of their program. This information exists based upon the success of Olympic and other programs, but probably has not been made widely available in a useful form. I believe that my next book entitled "The Coaches Manual of Sport Psychology" is desperately needed as a source to explain this information to coaches in a way that is concise, comprehensible and provides formats for including mental training that have shown to be productive over time. I would not be surprised if many parents may find this book a suitable present for their coach.

The fear of some coaches may be justified because in the distant past sport psychologists have created problems for them. The earliest use of sport psychologists was to deal with performance anxiety. The sport psychologist relaxed the players and they did better. It was mistakenly assumed that relaxing would be good for everyone, but it is not good for everyone and some athletes did worse. The reason, which is now known, is that relaxing some who did not need it took them to a lower level of arousal and out of their IPS. I would expect all Sport Psychologists to now know better than this, but competency in the field demands mastery of a large knowledge base and significant skills in application of the concepts, which varies between providers.

Coaches need to do the same work you need to do to be sure they have the right provider, but it is a challenge. I have worked with many coaches who had some knowledge of sport psychology that they used with their athletes, but would bring me in for more comprehensive or advanced training. We discussed a situation where I once worked with a Division I coach who had taken a sport psychology class in school. Although the team had no problems, she knew the value of sport psychology and asked me to provide mental training for the team. I trained them at home and then went to nationals with them with the result that her team tied for third, the best finish in school history in that sport. The following year she left the university and recommended to the next coach that she also include mental training. The new coach thought she knew more than she actually did, and included me only in a minimal and ineffective manner, despite my counsel that this was the wrong thing to do. The team, composed mostly of the same individuals, with a year more of experience, did very poorly at nationals and upon return told me they were not as strong mentally and wished I had been there.

In another instance a Clinical Sport Psychologist contacted the coach of a very talented and upcoming professional athlete in an individual sport and described the services offered. The coach informed the CSP that he was a sport psychologist, although he had no real qualifications, and that he knew what was needed. He prevented the CSP from speaking with the athlete. A year of so later it was learned that the player had been doing poorly for quite some time, had never reached their potential, and although quite young was considering retirement. The coach that prevented the CSP from working with the athlete was long gone, but the damage was done and the athlete was the one who paid the price for the coach's limitations.

I have worked with many great coaches at all levels who knew enough about sport psychology to realize the limitations of their knowledge, but unfortunately there are plenty of the other kind around at all levels. The most knowledgeable coaches were already doing smarter psychological things with their athletes, but knew enough to realize that they were only able to scratch the surface of what I could bring to their athletes. It is the coaches who are less advanced or more severely limited in their psychological knowledge, that are the least likely to incorporate a professional level of mental training into a program.

One of the best coaches I have ever worked with was Anatoli Nasarenko who was the former national team coach for the USSR, but became a coach for the US Army wrestling team after the Soviet Union break up. Although it was initially challenging for me to understand his relatively good English, our work together was extremely effective because mental training was such a large part of the tremendously successful Soviet sports programs and he understood clearly the role of the sport psychologist. He knew the mental focus that was critical to success, but also knew where coaching ended, and that I would be much more qualified to teach the athletes how to create that focus. We reviewed each athlete, he told me what he thought each needed to change or maximize in their mental approach, and then turned it over to me. As noted previously, the Army team we worked for went on to establish new military and Olympic records.

When you are reviewing the qualifications of sport psychology providers or even coaches who believe they can provide the sport psychology knowledge that your athlete needs, there are things you can review that will give you some insight into their true abilities. The following list of important concepts and questions may serve as a useful guide for evaluating the qualifications of someone seeking to provide services.

Guidelines:

1. Determine the type of sport psychology services you are seeking. Do a needs assessment with your child and identify their strengths and weaknesses. There may be several things that will be useful to your athlete so make a list of them all and rank order them. Maybe providing your athlete with a general mental training program

will give them what they need or there might be some specific areas of the mental game where you wish to provide more concentrated training. Every athlete needs to know the essential concepts and be using them correctly to get the most out of themselves and avoid problems. If they have no specific difficulties, then that might be all they need.

2. Use all sources available such as the internet and recommendations from coaches or other parents to identify potential providers.

3. Evaluate the credentials of potential providers. Look deeper than the surface when reviewing credentials and determine what actually was involved in their training. Some credentials can look good on the surface or be from an institution you recognize but that does not always mean that they had any kind of meaningful training. Feel free to ask them about their relevant background. I believe parents need to know that a provider is competent. I have no problem talking about my background and believe other providers should be equally as willing to discuss theirs.

4. When you have identified someone you think may be a good choice, contact them and talk to them. I try to always speak or communicate in some way to the athlete or parent before a first appointment to answer questions and assure a good match. The first part of my initial appointment, which usually includes the parents or coach if appropriate, is about reviewing the needs of the athlete and discussing the plan for addressing them. I suggest that your expect a provider to be able to explain the situation your child is in and the plan to work with them

in a way that makes sense to you by the end of the first hour. I do this all the time, so it is clearly possible, and think it is important for the athlete and parents to understand the situation and process. If a provider is unwilling or unable to do this, you may question why they are not able to provide this information and consider other options if you are not satisfied with the answer.

5. Discuss payment conditions ahead of time, most providers do not take insurance. Because I am a licensed clinical psychologist, some symptoms of stress in the situation that rise to the level of an adjustment disorder are sometimes covered by insurance and the parents may be able to get reimbursed for my services, this may be relevant for you. Although sport psychology services are not cheap, many sports clinics and other things that help athletes be successful are not cheap either. On balance, the bang for the buck in mental training is not bad considering that all short and long term success is dependent on the quality of the mental game. Remember, everything is created first in the mind.

6. Remember that although many types of educational training can be provided in a group setting at the educational level, eliminating specific conditions that hold the athlete back may require the higher expertise of a Clinical Sport Psychologist in an individual setting. To address specific needs such as competition anxiety, slumps, low confidence, apparent low effort, yips in golf or any of a wide range of performance issues, you will probably need the level of training and experience of a Clinical Sport Psychologist. Some issues come up frequently and for these you may be more likely to find a specialist. For

example, in the baseball community I have developed a reputation for getting athletes out of slumps quickly and have "affectionately" become known as Dr. Slump. Coaches who send me players have started to joke to the parents that I can get them out of slumps in one session, because it has happened. We all laugh about it because it seems absurd given that slumps in pitching and hitting have ruined careers. However, understanding the mental mechanics of a slump makes a big difference in dealing with them and allows me to show athletes why the slump is happening, and teach them how to get out in a relatively short period of time. As a result of understanding the mental mechanics of the process, players also develop a resistance to future slumps. Different sport psychologists have different training and experience so feel free to ask if they have had experience and success with the challenge you face. However, if a specialist is not available, a good Clinical Sport Psychologist may still be able to help you.

7. You should expect success. Although athletes differ regarding their ability to respond to training, you should generally be able to expect some changes in a few sessions. It is totally appropriate for you to inquire regarding progress being made. I am not suggesting that you be overly intrusive or demanding, but it is the right thing to do to ask the question. Some things do take longer to change, but you still should be able to get an answer from your sport psychologist that makes sense to you. I recently worked with a high school tennis player hoping to obtain a scholarship. She had been working with another sport psychologist with strong credentials for at

least six months with no significant improvement. The parents finally decided to try someone else and with agreement from the athlete, found me upon referral. The things the other sport psychologist was doing made no sense to me and I taught the her different things that I would expect to be helpful. Within three sessions or so she was feeling much more confident, and within a month completed nationals again without one instance of the problem she had continually struggled with for years. It was good the parents left when they did, but it would have been better if they had made the change earlier. A long period of no change or a process that does not feel right needs timely attention. Sometimes a different provider with a different approach makes a difference.

8. Ask the provider if they have worked with this age group of athletes in the sport your athlete plays. This should not be a deciding factor, but it may influence success. I have worked with almost every sport successfully although at some point it was the first time in that particular sport. The mental demands and mental training techniques to address these demands generalize across most sports so it is possible to be effective working with an athlete in a sport where the provider has had no previous experience. On the other hand, my extensive experience working with golf, tennis, baseball, basketball, soccer and football does help me be more effective more quickly in those sports.

I hope that I have not discouraged you from seeking a sport psychologist for mental training because a strong mental game is an absolute necessity if there is any expectation that an athlete will compete at the best of their ability, or have a chance of reaching their potential. Competing at the best of their ability is all we can hope for, and we certainly do not want any less. Some good sport psychology knowledge is better than none at all, and some can be gained from books. Unlike the past, these days many of the athletes with whom I work have read books on sport psychology. Although some information can be gained from books, just like coaching is irreplaceable to develop skills in a particular sport, there is no replacement for individual mental coaching from a good mental coach. This is true for the basic information on how to apply themselves most effectively, but it is much more critical to get immediate help with conditions that can damage or even bring an end to a sports career such as performance anxiety or slumps. Although these conditions can destroy their sports experience, assistance from a good sport psychologist can fairly quickly turn a demoralizing situation into one of newly found power and success.

Chapter 17

THE ROLE OF THE PARENT

Basic considerations

Almost every coach will tell you that the biggest problem they have in coaching is the parents. Parents who have inappropriately inserted themselves into the coaching and competition environment have created more damage to their child's progress and program than all other influences combined. Don't be one of those problem parents. It does not have to be that way and it is critical for you to get it right. Getting it right is discussed in this, and other chapters in this book. This is the time to engage your "smart mind" and evaluate your input accurately, including emotions and actions, and modify your behavior as needed to avoid significantly damaging your child's chance for success and maximally support their development.

One excellent coach I worked with put it very simply, "the role of the parent is to give kids what they need to be successful." This is certainly true, and I believe most parents try to do this, but it is not as simple as it used to be when we were growing up.

A traditional mountain climbing expedition provides a good analogy for the support structure needed by a young athlete today. For a major climb, after extensive planning and a significant investment of money has been committed, a large mountain assault support team with many specialties including medical, nutrition, guides and equipment is assembled. The support team that may number in the hundreds labors for many weeks to provide the chance for a small number of climbers, maybe even only one or two, to attempt the summit. Although partial radio contact is maintained, at some point, the climbers are on their own and the support team must just sit back and wait. The analogy is almost perfect for youth sports today.

The level of execution and competition in youth sports today is now much more demanding than ever before requiring a more sophisticated effort for the child to be competitive. It used to be that being a big kid would allow you to play football, but now you have to be big enough, fit and execute well just to play on a high school football team. Sometimes now a smaller more skilled athlete will play ahead of a much bigger athlete on a football team. In figure skating, jumps that could win the Olympics a few years ago are now commonly done in regional competitions. To enable an athlete to mount a competitive effort in sports now demands advanced support in many areas including: nutrition, physical training, additional coaching and mental training. More than once a parent has told me that doing what is needed for their athlete is like having a second job.

In the limited space in this book I have tried to address some of the most prevalent problems and challenges that parents face. Every child is different, every parent is different and every parent child system is a somewhat unique variation of the universal theme. Your challenge is to use the information in this book, and all other resources you can access, to create the parent role that will support your child in the most effective manner.

If you are confused about how to be the parent you wish to be in support of your child, if you have questions without answers, or lack confidence that the answers you have are the right ones, that's ok. Being the parent you want to be in support of your child is a process and no parent has the background to have all the answers at their fingertips. It is important to remember that it is not necessary to be a perfect parent and worrying about being a perfect parent is a source of additional stress. What is possible though is to be a "good enough parent", and that is all your child needs. Like we discussed in the case of your athlete, you can always be working to improve something, but along the way do not forget to appreciate what has been accomplished. Feeling good about what you already have done does not need to lead to satisfaction and complacency but can provide a type of fuel to help sustain the effort. However, remember the need to strike the right balance between being that interfering parent who creates problems for your coach and athlete, and being diligent to provide your athlete their best chance of success.

The demands on a parent fall into two categories: tactical and personal. The tactical demands include challenges in transportation, scheduling, equipment, nutrition and all the other resources needed by your athlete. Although the task of providing what your athlete needs can seem extensive, the personal demands can be an equal or greater challenge. Demands such as communication, problem solving and handling intense emotions can progress into unfamiliar territory for the parent as well as the child athlete. Parental response to both of these demands can have a significant impact on the ability of your child to compete at their best.

Overinvolvement

"The most damaging thing for the child is the unlived lives of the parent" was stated many years ago by the great Swiss Psychiatrist Carl Jung. Although Dr. Jung was not speaking about sports, we have seen this problem manifested repeatedly in numerous examples of parents acting badly and children suffering the consequences. Overinvolvement of parents is the source of many damaging situations that can interfere with children's success and enjoyment in sports. Involvement needs to be at the right level and focused correctly in several areas to create the kind of experience we want for our children.

Overinvolvement can take many forms but most examples we see fall into the two basic categories: emotional overinvolvement and tactical overinvolvement. Dr. Jung was speaking of emotional over involvement where the parent tends to live and experience their own life through the experiences of the child. In this situation, the parent feels many of the emotions the child does, but frequently at a more extreme level. Parents vary in the extent to which they have a full life of their own, but in the more extreme cases of overinvolvement the parent may get a significant amount of their pleasure and fulfillment in life from the sport experience of the child. In these situations parents can often be seen to be visibly nervous during competition and appear to live and die on the outcome. With overinvolvement the impact on the athlete is always negative. When the parent needs the athlete to do well to experience their own feelings of pleasure, the athlete inevitably experiences it as additional pressure. So here we have the irony that the more the parent needs the athlete do well, the more the athlete feels pressure which interferes with their ability to focus in practice and perform well in competition, resulting in the opposite effect. A term used recently to describe some of the signs indicting an overinvolved parent is the "helicopter parent" who hovers around the child and sport environment. There is an ideal quantity and type of involvement for the parent and although there are some generalities that can be applied, the specifics need to be identified for your specific situation. It is important to differentiate between the desirable state of parents enjoying, first hand and vicariously, the experience their child is having from an unhealthy state of need satisfaction of the parent through youth sport.

Tactical overinvolvement

Tactical overinvolvement is to some extent derived from emotional overinvolvement but is manifested more by actively meddling in the activities associated with the sport. It might be seen as the parent being more aware of schedules and processes of training than the athlete and constantly asking questions or taking the lead in scheduling. Tactical overinvolvement is also seen when the parent becomes very involved in coaching and is constantly interfering on and off the field. This might include continually contacting the coach with questions, suggestions or criticisms, or quizzing the athlete about why one thing is happening or why not other things. We see tactical overinvolvement where parents are yelling instructions to the child while they are actually playing, or even yelling at the coach for decisions made during the game.

As I have said, the parent needs to be involved but the point must be recognized where an action would be crossing the line and becoming overly involved to the detriment of the child. Interestingly, it is the child athlete who almost always becomes aware of the problem before the parent or coach. The child may not understand the entire situation, but they do know something is not right and suffer for it. In these situations the child is frequently embarrassed and often experiences problems from this situation until they finally have to go through the emotionally difficult process of asking the parent to not come to competition or practice. If it gets to that point, there has already been loss in the sport process so it is important to listen for more subtle things your athlete might say that might indicate their concern with some of your activities.

The bite of the Tiger Mom

If you wish to be a tiger mom, it is very important not to bite your own children. This should go without saying and although I am obviously speaking in metaphor here, you may also recall a story I saw in the news where a stage mother in a child beauty contest actually did bite her daughter. I believe the daughter bit the mother first, but is this surprising? Most parents do not actually bite their children, but I have seen a huge amount of short and long term harm to the athlete and the parent-child relationship that endured for many years, resulting from a very high demand and high pressure situation created by the parents.

The tiger mom concept has been in our awareness for the last couple of years after publication of a book by that name. At the point that the constellation of behaviors and beliefs commonly known as the tiger mom concept becomes a detriment to the welfare of the child, it is a good example of tactical overinvolvement. It should be noted that tactical overinvolvement may or may not have roots in emotional overinvolvement so it is important to review the situation completely if you have inclinations in this direction. The tiger mom concept has its roots in the desirability of what is known as the "Asian work ethic." In many individual sports Asian athletes have developed a reputation as very hard working and results often reward the hard work. The way many think about the tiger mom can be briefly described as a parent who pushes their child incessantly with practice and performance demands significantly higher than the norm. This often includes areas in addition to the primary sport. I completely support total commitment to whatever you are doing at the moment, and a good work ethic is irreplaceable, but when external pressure is taken too far it generally results in a lot of undesirable unintended consequences.

One problem caused by the tiger mom can be a switch within the athlete from internal to external motivation with the attendant problems discussed in the chapter on motivation, but there are many others. Although the tiger mom extreme pressure might result in more activity and may appear beneficial from some vantage points, the overall results I have observed have never been good and frequently resulted in creating problems. Frequent symptoms observed in kids pushed by tiger moms or tiger fathers include uncharacteristic increases in irritability, anxiety, unexplained fatigue, depression, eating disorders, self mutilation, significant negative attitudes of the athlete toward them self and a general increase in conflict between the parents and child. I frequently see athletes damaged by tiger moms, or dads, displaying several of these symptoms. Many have lost interest in a sport they previously loved and want to quit just to get away from the pressure.

Interestingly, some of the problems created by tiger mom characterized by high pressure demands can be seen as the result of ignoring one of the most valuable concepts in the Asian culture, the importance of balance. One client of mine was a teenage girl of Asian heritage in an individual sport. She was a delightful person and her mother was also very nice. I never met her father who was always gone on business. This young girl was in a gifted program in a high pressure private school and drove herself incessantly toward perfection in all things. She did not have many friends because she did not have time. The result was poor performance in her sport below her abilities and physical symptoms her doctor said were stress related. Her mother said she did not push her daughter and had tried to get the girl to not put so much pressure on herself. I tried to get the girl to ease back and reach for balance. She overtly and completely refused, with undesirable consequences as a result. The fact is some kids will do it to themselves without the influence of their parents and coaches. A limited viewpoint and approach can only lead to limited results and the outcome in this case was not good.

A child is not a smaller version of an adult. Children need certain things to develop normally. Children need time to develop social skills with their friends during childhood, which is difficult to make up later. Children also need time to just be kids. It is important to build in time for free play, which is not wasted time but has many developmental benefits. The child needs free time to explore and discover who they are and what they like. Results are very clear that no athlete will get to the highest levels of achievement without a good work ethic and significant motivation. But, we must remember that the biggest losses in sports come from a mental breakdown of process such that the athlete can not use the skills they already possess to their highest ability. As we have previously discussed, the dominant reason athletes suffer mental dysfunction in sports is pressure. It is well known that the biggest reason talented kids do poorly, unaccountably seem to lose interest, and leave sports is due to the impact of too much pressure and emphasis on competition. The best way to avoid this is to understand the experience of your child, be mindful of your feelings, evaluate the results of your input and create a balance that is ideal for your child.

To be clear, I am a proponent of total commitment and maximum effort in training and competition. Creating a work ethic of total commitment and maximum effort that is part of an approach that is balanced with the other needs of your athlete is a very important part of giving your child the opportunity to reach their potential as an athlete and as a person. If the parent maximizes the factors that contribute to success at the right level, many of which are discussed in this book, then the parent can just sit back and enjoy the journey of their athlete through the sport experience.

Emotional overinvolvement

Over the last few years, we have seen many examples in the news of emotional overinvolvement with parents losing emotional control and causing fights with other parents, running on the field to assault officials and even killing a coach. These are the extreme examples that make the news but you may recall examples where you have seen parents behaving badly and being banned from competition, or at the least causing embarrassment for their children.

James I. Millhouse, Ph.D.

Many children have less enjoyable and successful sport experiences, and have even quit a sport, due to the fact that one or more of their parents were overinvolved at the emotional level.

Emotional involvement can be a difficult or confusing situation for parents but it is clear that the correct type and level of parent involvement is crucial to success. Do your best to evaluate the level of your emotional involvement and make adjustments or seek help as needed. One of the hardest things for people to do has always been to objectively evaluate themselves. The first place you may look for information is with any extremely strong feelings you experience. Strong feelings may be an indication of a problem, or they may not. Sometimes problems are contained in more subtle feelings or expectations, you never know, but the key is to gather a wide range of information about this situation if you have a concern. If you seek feedback from your athlete, coach or even other parents you may be surprised by the volume of information you will obtain. You may know that courage is a valuable commodity in many areas in sport. The same is sometimes true in the role of the parent where it might be challenging to honestly evaluate your feelings and make adjustments to your involvement. This may be difficult but the welfare and success of your child is at stake, and remember any expectation that you should be perfect is unreasonable. Everyone who cares is on a journey to become better than before, and it is what we do on the journey that becomes our life, which can be awesome and fulfilling, while still less than perfect.

It may be helpful to remember that problematic overinvolvement is never intended by the parent to be the problem it becomes, but it is easy to slide into, and tactical overinvolvement is usually

214

motivated by a positive desire to help create the best experience possible. This is one reason for the resistance seen when a parent is given feedback about a troubling behavior. It is natural to want our children to do well, to be successful, and it is easy to feel sadness if they fail to reach goals they want very much. However, the more you can hold the ideal philosophical and emotional perspective for your child, and interact with coaches and others in the environment in the most effective way, the easier it will be for your child to succeed. In a problematic or tense situation, remember that there can be many solutions. If things start going bad, step back for a moment and rethink the situation. It is almost assured that when a situation is fully reviewed, discussed and obvious changes made, that a constructive solution can be found.

Developing your own IPS

For a parent to be of maximum help to their child in sport, there is an ideal perspective and level of the primary parental factors that influence the success of your child. These factors include; philosophy of sport and competition, your emotional responses, your ability to respond to the thoughts and feelings of your athlete, communication with your athlete and coaches, supervision of the situation and administrative or tactical functions. I can give you ideas, arguments and tools that have value, but it is up to you to decide what works best for you and your child.

Recalling our discussion of the Ideal Performance State which was defined as the collection of factors from which the athlete will perform their best, we could consider the most desirable set of factors for the parent as their Ideal Performance State, or Ideal Performance Strategy, that will provide the best support to their athlete. As with the athlete, the IPS is something you shoot for as a parent realizing that none are ever perfect and any can be improved. Remember to take credit and feel good about what you have done well, in addition to identifying things you would like to improve. It may help to see the task of developing the IPS for yourself as a parent as a strategy to develop the right type of support structure for your athlete.

So feel free to use any of the ideas, lists and guidelines provided in this book to assess the sport experience of your child for information on your role. You may want to talk to other parents, you child or coaches about what you find or changes you think may be desirable. But remember, that although some things might be the same for all the athletes, such as sport demands or basic mental mechanics, many of the personal specifics for each athlete may be different. For this reason, your parent strategy for optimal involvement to help your athlete achieve the highest level of their potential may have some differences from that of other parents.

Developing the ideal parent strategy is a progressive endeavor. You may wish to write down the goals you have for your child and then develop a list of steps in your strategy that support their effort to achieve them. There is information all through this book that you can use to develop your ideal strategy but the following lists may provide some helpful ideas.

Red flags that may, but do not necessarily, signal overinvolvement by a parent can include:

1. The parent pressuring the child to do too much.
2. Yelling in anger or swearing at the child's games, performance or practice.

3. Feeling embarrassed by the child's performance.
4. Getting in physical altercations with the child, other parents, coaches or officials.
5. Constantly reminding the child of assignments and goals set by the parent or coach. They should take primary responsibility but you can help.
6. Betting on the outcomes of the child's sports.
7. Letting aspects of the child's sport distract the parent from other responsibilities such as those of a spouse, provider for the family or other children.

Review of problems created by pressure

Each child will have an ideal level of parent support that works best for them and a good way to figure this out is to ask them for their input. Problems can be created by excessively pressuring kids which may include:

1. Pressure and too much competitive focus spoil the fun in sports for kids. This is the main reason kids with great potential quit while young, lose interest in their sport, exhibit lack of motivation, perform poorly and get in conflicts other kids and with parents.
2. External pressure changes motivation from internal to external which can cause a reduction of internal motivation and less control by the athlete. External motivation can have some value but also caries significant risk and must be used carefully.
3. Pressure to win focuses athletes on the end product or outcome, rather than on what they need to focus on to be successful, which is to be in the present and focus on execution.

4. Expectations that feel like demands to do well can lead kids to put pressure on themselves and experience unpleasant feelings if they believe they have disappointed a parent or coach. Do not underestimate the tendency of young athletes to be concerned about disappointing others.

5. Pressure to perform is a major source of competitive anxiety and under performing which can also lead to other emotional and behavioral issues.

Guidelines for emotional involvement

Guidelines and tips for the creating the right level of involvement and providing emotional support include:

1. It is good for kids to be as involved in decision making and other tasks associated with their sport as much as possible. This encourages them to take ownership and feel like it is their sport and about them, opposed to something parents are creating for them or for the parents.

2. Do not be over concerned with failure. Kids need to learn to deal with failure and it is the greatest teacher of that which we have not mastered. Every great athlete knows how to deal with failure, or they never would become great.

3. Balance the desire for greatness with appreciation for what is achieved. Focusing significantly on what good has been achieved fuels the engine to continue, in other words it can support motivation by feeling successful.

4. Don't rant about the situation or be critical of the coach in front of kids; it can damage the kid's attitude and their ability to respond appropriately to the coach.

5. Don't accept that you need to be a "basket case" at a game or that other disturbing emotions are "just a necessary part of the process." Feelings that are unmanageable tell you that you need to look at your perspective that is responsible for the feelings and evaluate the possibility of change.

6. Help kids believe if they tried their hardest that they can be proud of the effort and live with the results. Help them understand how success is created and appreciate that success is a result of achieving many goals along the path to creating the execution that results in success. It is ok to try your hardest and fail, that is the best way to develop the most quickly. Remind them that failures teach us as much and usually more than success, especially when we are trying our hardest. This point is critical.

7. Do not over interpret or over react if your kid doesn't play. There can be many reasons they are not playing so take the time to learn the reason before you respond to the situation.

8. Do not be overly critical of mistakes. Be supportive of the effort if mistakes are made and help kids realize mistakes are a necessary and natural part of getting better. Kids know if they have made a mistake so don't rub it in but be supportive and help them see mistakes in the proper perspective. Punishing mistakes intentionally or even unintentionally can reduce the fun, decrease motivation and inhibit taking risks that usually are necessary for improvement.

9. If pressure is being experienced it may be helpful for both the parent and athlete to remember the thought that it's only a game. Even if the truth is that success

does have consequences such as awards or scholarships, this thought may still contribute to the most productive focus for creating the best performance of which they are capable.

10. Remember to practice open minded listening with your kids and do not let your emotions influence their communication. Their experience of the sport holds the keys to improving execution. Regardless of what you know to be right or wrong, you must link up to the athlete at their level of understanding to most effectively lead them to considering other options. This is called pacing.

11. Do not let them define themselves in narrow terms such as a basketball player and the like. Sports should be something they do, not who they are. You may want to foster the idea of them as a person first and a player second. When you observe almost all champions, at least the happiest and most consistently successful, you will find a person with a balanced view of competition and them self as a person.

12. Similarly, do not let the kid's entire self worth come only from sport just as your emotional happiness cannot come from the sport. It is better to have their self worth come from a number of sources and particularly internal characteristics, values and choices over which they have complete control.

13. Avoid living through your children and don't let your emotions be dictated by your kid's actions or outcomes, including those of the team. If parents live and die on their kid's performance, the kids feel responsible for their parent's feelings and are distracted. As discussed before,

listen to feedback from others including your athlete. Remember, most overinvolved parents do not think they are. This blindness to one's own state is the norm, so a specific effort to think outside the box of your own mind and use outside feedback to assess your involvement is a wise choice.

Guidelines for tactical involvement

I have been using the term tactical support to include all things other than understanding feelings and providing the right kind of emotional environment and support. Guidelines that may help you maximize the effectiveness of your tactical support include:

1. Gather the information from coaches and other sources about what your kid needs to be successful. Understand the specific demands and risks of the sport.

2. See if the coach fosters the type of environment you appreciate, not necessarily the same in all ways, but not contradictory in important ways. If you feel concern, communicate with the coach with the understanding they have their own reasons for what they do and try for a comprehensive understanding before you reach conclusions.

3. Be supportive of every aspect of what kids need and make resources available as much as possible. Try not to let antiquated thinking interfere with progress.

4. Help the kid appreciate honest feedback and not resist useful information.

5. Make sure you are on the same page as your kid and the coach.

6. Help your kid build an appropriate relationship with the coach, ideally with trust, open and accurate communication.

7. Be realistic about what to expect regarding the abilities of your child and where they fit into the team while being supportive of potential for improvement. Just because they were a big fish in a small pond, they might not also have the resources to be the same kind of big fish in a big pond. They need to experience their value in what ever pond and what ever role they are in. This is very important.

8. Understand why injuries occur. Be wary of overuse injuries in children which are more prevalent when they specialize at an early age. Investigate reasonable adjustments to their program if injuries are frequent or seem unnecessary.

9. Develop a trusting relationship with the coach, and trust them to do the right thing after you are comfortable with their approach. Trust but continue to monitor.

10. Balance monitoring everything with not being intrusive.

11. Do not think your little angel can do no wrong.

12. Support internal motivation and keep external rewards in perspective.

13. Keep kids focused on action in the present. Good present creates good performance and the best future outcome possible.

14. Monitor your child's feelings to see if they continue to have fun, by the definition that makes sense to you and them. As we discussed in the essential concepts fun, reward and achievement can have many meanings dependent on the athlete and situation.

15. Be generally positive while you foster a good work ethic.

16. Encourage and facilitate a constructive response to low performance, use it as a tool to learn something valuable, not as evidence of being a failure. You may need to remind them that failing at something does not make us a failure as a person.

17. Model good sportsmanship with an appreciation for good effort.

18. Identify good role models such as professionals or others of the same age that demonstrate the values, perspective and attitude that you consider healthy.

19. Remember, whenever referring to other athletes as models make sure your child will not take it as a comparison where they feel inferior, shamed or less valued by you. Generally be wary of comparing your athlete to their peers because there are many opportunities for your athlete to use the comparison in a harmful way, even though that was not your intent.

20. Keep in mind the very important fact that your athlete might not perceive things like you do or the way you expect them to. Make it a practice to use listening skills effectively to differentiate your thoughts and feelings from what they are perceiving, thinking and feeling about things.

Parent care and support

I was walking through the gym one day when I was coaching gymnastics and a group of the team kid's parents approached me with the question, "what about us." They had seen the change in their kids who had gone from nervous and stressed in competition to calm and focused, and wanted me to teach them the same thing. I did teach them a relaxation procedure they found helpful in reducing stress, but did not have the time to help them understand how they could see the situation differently and avoid the stress completely. It is my hope that this book will provide assistance to that end, but the point is that it is also important for the parent to take care of their own physical and emotional health. As we previously discussed, it is not necessary for the parent to be stressed out or struggle emotionally at competitions. Although it is common, it is neither an inevitable or desirable part of the process.

The role of sport parent has technical, tactical and emotional challenges that are all a potential source of stress. The way you face these challenges can have a significant impact on you, your family as well as your child.

When a captain takes a ship into battle he tries to go in with it in the best shape possible. It is the same for you. It is important to maintain yourself with sleep, nutrition, exercise, emotional support, possibly time for yourself and whatever else you need to function well.

If a tactical situation is very difficult, use your creativity to find a better solution rather than just carry on and be drained. If you have difficulty dealing with interpersonal or emotional parts of the process, solutions can be found, get help if you need it. For some parents, using relaxation techniques at competitions results in a much more enjoyable experience. With the understanding that our beliefs and thoughts create our feelings, you may be able to find a philosophy or set of beliefs that create the feelings and experience of competition that will be best for you and your child. Although I have alluded to the value of philosophy and existential beliefs when describing some of the strategies athletes have based their solutions on, a more complete look into these areas is beyond the scope of this book.

If you find yourself struggling with any part of the experience, whether it is tactical demands that have become burdensome or if the emotional demands are making the process difficult, it is very important to know that there is a better solution, and also that it is very important to find it. If you think "I will just tough it out," that solution, although better than some, has not appeared to work very well in the past. To make matters worse, remember that your kids are watching. We have all seen children embarrassed by their parents, but even more important, children take cues of all types regarding how to handle situations from their parents. When they see you responding to pressure situations with ease, it shows them that they can do it too. This learning occurs at the conscious level but probably even more important, they gain the unconscious belief that it can be done.

As we have previously discussed, the level of performance necessary for a young athlete to be successful today in serious competition and the implications of success are much higher than in the past. This sets the stage for high pressure and stress. Although we often see unpleasant feelings around sports, it is not necessary, or desirable, for these feelings to persist. I have seen too many parent and child systems with stress and troubling emotions that could have been changed to situations of happiness and reward, if a solution had been effectively sought. With an understanding of the factors involved, and an effective role created by the parent, the whole process can unfold fairly easily and set everyone on a course to have an enjoyable and rewarding experience.

Going forward

At the beginning of this book I stated that my intent was to discuss the relevant factors impacting your kid in sports and give you tools you could use to help them be more effective in reaching their goals. Looking back, I believe I accomplished that goal. However, it is up to you to use this information correctly. Remember, this book is a guide to make sure everyone is moving in the right direction, but everyone's path will be a little different based on individual and situational differences.

Unfortunately, those parents, and coaches for that matter, who most need to change their destructive behavior, are those least likely to read this book, either because they think they already know everything or just don't care. We have all seen those parents who aggressively and selfishly pursue what they think is best for their child to the detriment of others around them, although this method eventually backfires. We have also seen coaches who, for a number of reasons, conduct their program in a way that is detrimental to some or all of their athletes. I hope this book has given you sufficient information to recognize those behaviors and see a platform from which to confront them if their behaviors are detrimental to your child. I could write a more complete and detailed book for the parent to address the issues discussed in this book, but I doubt that many people would take the time to read it. So, unless there is sufficient demand to explore the topics discussed in greater depth, I will assume that this book provides sufficient guidance.

Writing this book it has become abundantly clear that although coaches universally know that the mind is a critical factor in performance, most of them, even good coaches, do not understand the appropriate role of mental training in a sports program or how to use a sport psychologist. Because the need is so great, I plan to expedite the writing of another book, the Coaches Manual of Sport Psychology, that will provide this information and be available within six months. As I mentioned before, you may think of the coaches book as a great present for your coach.

There are many books about sport psychology available to athletes so it has been my belief that another one was not needed. However, it has become clear that no other books deal with the same material presented in this book such that they can serve as an adequate substitute. Many parents will give this book to their athlete to read for the essential concepts, which is a great idea. However, I have decided to expedite a book for athletes with a deeper discussion of the essential concepts, and more examples, that should make the parents' job of educating their child in the information they need to know a little easier.

The fact is, that most of the parents who bring their children to me are mostly on the right track and are enjoying the sport experience with their kids. Just remember, you do not have to be a perfect parent, only a "good enough" parent, to give them what they need to develop an approach to training and competition that will enable them to reap the rewards of their efforts. This will help them to not only create success in the short term, but also to establish an effective approach they can use to create success for the rest of their life, in any venue they choose.